Learning the Math Facts

With the Broken Number Line Method

Joseph Strayhorn, Jr.

Psychological Skills Press

Copyright Joseph Strayhorn, 2016

Psychological Skills Press

205 Willard Way, Ithaca, NY 14850

www.psychologicalskills.org

ISBN: 978-1-931773-21-8

Table of Contents

Introduction: To the Instructor..6
Chapter 1: Why Learn Math Facts Well?..12
Chapter 2: How You Learn To Do Something Well................................14
Chapter 3: It's Important to See How Big the Numbers Are..................18
Chapter 4: Ideas That Let Us Memorize Fewer Addition Facts.............22
    Order doesn't make a difference..22
    Adding 0..23
    Adding 1..23
    Adding 10..24
    How much memorizing have we now saved?....................................25
Chapter 5: Practicing Adding With Ordinary Number Lines.................27
Chapter 6: Adding Using Broken Number Lines....................................29
    Broken number lines for addition facts..31
    Adding a whole row with broken number lines................................35
    The Broken Number Line Page for Addition....................................38
Chapter 7: Ideas for Reducing Memorization in Subtraction................39
    Subtraction is the opposite, (or inverse) of addition.........................39
    Subtracting 0, and subtracting a number from itself........................40
    Subtracting 1, and subtracting the number just before a number........41
    Subtracting 10 from a number in the range from 11 to 19................41
    Subtracting the number in the ones' place from a number from 11 to 19..41
    Practice using these rules...42
Chapter 8: Subtracting Using Ordinary Number Lines..........................43
Chapter 9 : Subtracting Using Broken Number Lines............................45
    Broken number line page for addition and subtraction....................50
Chapter 10: Fact Families, and dominoes to Show Them......................51
Chapter 11: Optional: One More Way of Visualizing Addition and Subtraction..58
Chapter 12: Practicing Addition and Subtraction Facts with Numerals..61

- Adding and subtracting 0 and 1 62
- The Plus 10's 62
- The Plus 2's 63
- The Doubles 65
- The One Aparts 66
- The Plus 9's 68
- The Plus 8s 69
- The Two Aparts 70
- The Make 10s and Their Siblings 71
- More drill on addition and subtraction with the basic 36 families 72

Chapter 13: Addition Work That's Useful for Multiplication 75
- Review of regrouping or "carrying" when adding 75
- Regrouping when subtracting, or "borrowing" 76
- The skip-counting sequences 76

Chapter 14: Four Rules That Cut Down on Memorization in Multiplication 82
- Order doesn't make a difference in multiplication 82
- Multiplying by zero 84
- Multiplying by one 84
- Multiplying by 10 85
- Practicing with some of the multiplication facts we've left out 86

Chapter 15: Multiplying Using an Ordinary Number Line 87
Chapter 16: Multiplying Using Broken Number Lines 88
Chapter 17: Division, and Its Relation to Multiplication 97
Chapter 18: Reducing Memorization Of Division Facts 101
- Fact Families 101
- Dividing 0 by any number, and not dividing by 0 101
- Dividing by 1, and dividing a number by itself 102
- Dividing numbers ending in 0 by 10 102
- Dividing numbers ending in 0 from 10 to 90 by the number in the tens' place 102

Chapter 19: Multiplication and Division Fact Families 104

Chapter 20: Multiplication Fact Families Using Broken Number Line Arrays..108
Chapter 21: Visualizing Multiplication Facts With The Traditional Multiplication Table...125
Chapter 22: Practicing Multiplication and Division Facts Using Numerals Only...129
Chapter 23: Practice With Random Math Facts...................................135
Index..139

Introduction: To the Instructor

When your student can effortlessly and accurately rattle off the basic facts of addition, subtraction, multiplication, and division, you will have reason to celebrate a very big accomplishment. The rest of the student's mathematics education will be much more pleasant and successful because of this accomplishment.

One of the major principles of education is what we call "hierarchy-ology." We can arrange learning tasks in order of difficulty. With any given student, at any given moment, we should work on the tasks that are not too hard, not too easy, but just right in their level of difficulty. Suppose we try to teach math facts by giving students lots of them to answer. What are students supposed to do when they don't know the answers? Very often, the challenge is frustrating and unpleasant. This book presents ways to make it easier to say math facts correctly. When students have built up skills with the easier methods, then, and only then, are they ready to go to the harder challenges.

There are several ways of making math facts easier. They include:
1. providing a visual aid,
2. going in order,
3. keeping family members together, and
4. practicing with smaller batches.

Let's talk about what each of these means.

I very much like the visual aid that I've called the "broken number line." I didn't use this in school, nor have I seen it used in any other curriculum, although I feel sure that others must have independently discovered it. One of the goals of early math education that it helps with is "number sense": having a gut feeling for how big numbers are. With a broken number line like this, for example,

Introduction: To the Instructor

```
1  2  3  4  5
6  7  8  9  10
```

you can represent 5+3 by seeing 5 numbers on the top row, and counting off 3 more as we continue on the bottom row, and land on 8. The numbers from 1 through 8 constitute 8 actual things, and seeing them teaches us how big 8 is, as well as helping us remember the addition fact. Being able to look under the 3 on the top row, rather than count three jumps on an ordinary number line, helps us to answer 5+3 faster. The advantage of the broken number line grows bigger when we get to larger sums such as 9+8.

Similarly, when we multiply, we can create arrays that show us how big the numbers are that we are dealing with. For example,

```
Row 1:      1  2  3  4
Row 2:      5  6  7  8
Row 3:      9  10 11 12
```

shows three rows, with four "things" (four numbers) in each row. We see three rows, we see 4 columns, and we see 12 things. Again, we're not just memorizing that 3 x 4 = 12; we're getting a gut feeling for how big the numbers are. We're getting a visual image of 3x4=12.

What do we mean by "going in order"? Suppose the student is looking at the number line broken at 5 above. The student says, "5+1=6; 5+2=7; 5+3=8; 5+4=9; 5+5=10." It's a lot easier to know that 5+3=8 when only a second before you've noted that 5+2=7. The preceding fact helps with the subsequent fact. For this reason, we first drill in order before drilling in random order.

Keeping family members together means, for example, taking advantage of the fact that 12-9=3 is much easier when you've just said that 9+3=12. For this reason, we often ask the student to say fact families like: 9+3=12; 3+9=12; 12-9=3; 12-3=9. Similarly, for multiplication and division, we ask for families such as 5x2=10; 2x5=10; 10/5=2; 10/2=5.

This book is meant to take your student through a series of steps toward math fact mastery, where each step is not much harder than the previous one. For this reason, I hope your journey is pleasant -- because your student's journey is pleasant.

I recommend starting at the beginning and going in order through the various explanations and exercises. If your student can read well enough that the two of you can take turns reading the paragraphs of explanatory material aloud to each other, you can use this book as a reading exercise as well as a math exercise. If your student can't read well enough, you can read the explanations to the student.

If your student knows addition and subtraction really well, but is shaky on multiplication and division, you can breeze quickly over the addition and subtraction parts -- or vice versa. A fairly high fraction of students that I've encountered, however, can use work in all four operations.

You and your student can take turns doing the "reflections exercise" with the explanatory paragraphs: you say something like, "This paragraph said that...." and you fill in what you got out of it. When you undertake this, which is a great method for learning anything that's written down, show the student how to do it. Model for the student how to summarize the paragraph in your own words. After hearing you do it, the student is much more ready to do it.

My inclination is not to time the student in any given exercise until the student has practiced enough to be able to do the exercise with complete accuracy, and the exercise is just starting to get easy enough to be boring. At this point, you can time the exercise and ask the student to do it several times, seeing how much the speed picks up.

Some students will come to you with very strong conditioned aversions to being timed on math facts. Some of them have had repeated experiences of being given a sheet of math facts they don't know, being asked to do them at great speed, and being negatively compared with other students who can do them better. Some of them may have been humiliated by being asked math fact questions they don't know, in front of other students who are ready with bullying derision or humiliating pity. If your student has a conditioned aversion, plan carefully. Make sure that all the student's experiences, and especially the first ones, are successes. If the student has an aversion to being timed, let the student work untimed and informally notice whether the student is getting faster.

When you do time, there are two ways: one is for a fixed time, such as a minute, or five minutes, or whatever you pick. If the student reaches the end of the list of problems before the time is up, the student starts immediately back at the beginning of the set. The second timing method is to keep going for a fixed number of questions, and then to divide the number of correct answers by the number of seconds and to multiply by 60 to get the rate, in correct answers per minute. You may want to practice with figuring out the number of correct answers per minute using each of these methods, so that you can do it quickly with your student.

It's good to time your student on the page where the answers are provided for 36 addition facts, to see how fast the student can get the answers out when they are provided and all the student has to do is to read them. You can time once for reading out the answers only (i.e., "4, 5, 6, 6, 7..." and another time for saying the whole fact (e.g. "two plus two, four; three plus two, five....") Some students can get words out of their mouths quicker than others. However fast the student can talk, you eventually want the student to be able to say the math facts that fast. (With practice, many students can learn to talk faster, also!)

A rough standard is over 60 facts per minute (one per second) for saying the answer only, and over 30 per minute (one every two seconds) for saying the question and answer. When saying the question and answer you can go faster by leaving out the word "equals." You can save a couple of syllables and go faster with division by saying "over" rather than "divided by" for something like 28/7.

Even though I mention timing, there's another metric of accomplishment: points. I recommend using a tally counter when working on math facts. (Cost of a tally counter is in the region of $5.) I recommend giving one click to the tally counter every time the student answers one question in any of the exercises. (A fact family of four deserves four clicks.) I recommend keeping a cumulative tally of how many points the student has done, from the very beginning of the endeavor. It's important to celebrate milestones of points -- 1000, 5000, etc. For some students at some or all parts of the process, it may be much better psychologically to focus on the total number of points accumulated than to focus on speed.

One of your big jobs is to decide how many times to do a certain exercise before moving on to the next one. Such a decision is at the heart of the artistry of teaching. When in doubt, I recommend that you err on the side of relaxing and accumulating more points and repeating exercises rather than trying to move ahead too quickly. Please let the student know from the very beginning that you don't just go from start to finish in this book and do everything once. (I try to let the student know this also, in Chapter 2!)

Suppose you want the student to drill on the plus 8's, in order. Should you ask the student to do this for one minute? five minutes? 50 points? 150 points? This too is part of the artistry of teaching. You have to determine how much stamina your student has. You want to talk with your student about building mental stamina, and getting capable of drilling for longer and longer periods of time without stopping.

The mistake that is so often made in education is to put too much pressure on the student to perform quickly, but to drill for very short periods of time, and to get very few "points" worth of practice in. If you celebrate the achievement of lots and lots of points, and push the total higher and higher, and really celebrate your student's getting more and more points per session, your student has a much greater chance of achieving mastery.

On the other hand, you want to avoid pushing the student to keep drilling beyond his or her work capacity too soon. Math facts drill is hard mental work. Just as you wouldn't ask a beginning track runner to go for 5 miles on the first day, you need to pick point totals to shoot for that are not too many, not too few, but just right, and you gradually increase as your student gets in better and better shape with regard to mathematical work capacity.

What if the student can't make the jump between saying facts with a visual aid, and looking away from the page and saying the facts without looking? Research into math facts education suggests that cutting down the total number of facts that the student drills on at any given time may be the answer. You don't want to overload the memory buffer. So, for example, rather than drilling on all the "9 times" facts, you may want to drill on just the first 5, and save the last 4 for another session. Or you may want to divide them up into 3 sets of 3. You will probably need to downsize the chunks a lot less if the student has done lots and lots of drill while looking at the visual aid, while you click the tally counter for a longer and longer time.

For some students at some times you will want to give positive feedback after every single fact, for every single click of the tally counter. "Right! Good! Yes!" and so forth, you say, communicating your true joy that your student is getting right answers. At other times you will want to let the student go to the end of the drill without interruption, so as to let the student speed along at maximum rate. When in doubt, reinforce, and do so enthusiastically. If the student finds the reinforcement annoying or distracting, don't hesitate to postpone it until the exercise goal (the time, or the point total) has been met. Then you can burst out the celebration you've been holding inside!

As you use this program with your student, please keep in mind that the student is learning more than math facts. The student is learning that big goals can be accomplished by lots of sessions of practice and work. Also, the student hopefully learns that work at the right level of difficulty can be pleasant. The student hopefully gets pleasant memories of success experience after success experience, and thus develops a positive association with both mathematics and with academic work in general. These are very important accomplishments.

Chapter 1: Why Learn Math Facts Well?

By math facts, I mean things like 6+9=15, 17-8=9, 6 x 7=42, and 64/8 =8. (In this book we use the / sign to mean "divided by." We'll sometimes use *, the asterisk, to mean "multiplied by," as most computer languages do.) For addition and multiplication, we're talking about the problems you can make with one-digit numbers, those from 0 through 9 (with 10 often thrown in as well). For subtraction and division, we're talking about the problems that are in the same "families" as those one digit addition and multiplication facts. (We'll talk later about what "fact families" are.)

What does it mean to know math facts well? It means that you don't have to count on your fingers, make a number line, reason out the answer, or even think very much -- you can just say the answer automatically. You can say the answers quickly and confidently. You know the facts so well that they don't distract you from whatever else you need to concentrate on in a math problem. First priority is to get the answers right, and second priority is to know them very quickly. You want to be able to look at a page of them and rattle off the answers just about as fast as you can get the words out of your mouth.

You can use this skill to help you make decisions in real life. Lots of the sorts of problems you find in math books are good examples of real-life decisions. Sadie has $14. She wants to buy some gloves that cost $9 and some socks that cost $7. Can she get both, and if not, how much more does she need to save? Dave is driving to Newfield, 80 miles away. He figures he'll be able to average about 40 miles an hour. What time does he have to leave to get to a meeting, if he wants to be there at 3 p.m.? People run into choice points like this in real life all the time.

If you work in a field like science, engineering, computing, accounting, construction, or several other jobs, math problems come up even more frequently, perhaps throughout each working day. For many people, doing math well makes the difference between earning a living and not! If you know math facts well, you can often estimate answers much more quickly than someone can get them with a calculator or computer. And even if you use a calculator or computer, you can check to make sure your answers make sense.

Even if you were to use math only in school and not in real life, it would still be a good idea to get very fast and accurate at math facts. School keeps going for many years, and most of those years include a math course and perhaps also a science course involving math. Math is much, much more enjoyable if you don't have to reach for a calculator or computer every time you're faced with 24/8 or 14-9. People who do well in math, and who like it, tend to be fast and accurate at the math facts.

When you do algebra and other higher forms of math, things are much easier and more pleasant if you can recall math facts quickly and accurately. For example, having a bunch of algebra problems of certain types can be like fun puzzles if you know the math facts well. If you don't, the same sorts of problems can really spoil your day.

You are probably going to get either homework or classwork or a test in math almost every school day for years. Close to every one of those exercises will be more pleasant and successful if you invest the time and energy necessary to know the math facts super-well.

In summary, knowing math facts can help you make decisions well, be successful in a job, and be happier and more successful in school!

Chapter 2: How You Learn To Do Something Well

To learn to do almost anything well, you have to practice, many, many times, doing the same thing, over and over, trying to do it better and better each time, and hopefully having fun doing it!

How many times has a golf champion practiced putting? How many times has a dancer practiced standard dance moves? How many times do experts at anything practice the same thing over and over?

Stephen Curry (an expert basketball player) was asked how many practice shots he took per day. He said: "It's not a ridiculous number. I count makes, so in the summer, I make 500. During the season, depending on what portion of the schedule we're going through, I make 200 to 350. And whatever goal I set before the workout is the goal. I won't shortcut it. If I play Around the World, I have to make 10 out of 13 at each of the seven spots to move on. If I don't, I'll sit at that same spot until I do."

Yo Yo Ma, who has a reputation as the world's best cello player, has been reported to practice and play about 2,000 hours a year, or between 5 and 6 hours a day, every day, and he has done this for several decades.

I don't expect you to put in that kind of time on math facts! But the point is that in order to get really skilled at something, you have to be willing to practice the same thing, over and over. Many students that I've seen have been irritated when asked to do the same exercise for even the second time, saying, "But I've already done this!" Yes, but they have not done it well enough. Or maybe they have done it well enough, but they need to practice so they can keep doing it well enough!

Let's define a phrase: *repetition-tolerance*. If after rehearsing a song once and doing fairly well, a musician says, "I've done it now, and it would be boring to do the same thing over again," that musician has little repetition-tolerance. If after rehearsing once, the musician thinks, "That was pretty good; I think I can do it even better," or "That was about perfect; let's see if I can do it again," or "I like the way that sounded; let me hear it again!" and keeps rehearsing over and over, that musician has much more repetition-tolerance. The second is likely to become a much, much better musician!

I read a study finding that for surgeons doing a certain type of operation, patients didn't do as well if they picked a surgeon who did the procedure only once or twice a year. If they picked a surgeon who did the operation more than 25 times a year, the patients did lots better.

So the first thing to remember about getting really skilled at something is: develop repetition-tolerance for practice. Be able to practice the same thing over and over. If you can't do this, get tougher until you can!

The second thing to remember is that when you practice, you don't just mindlessly do one more boring repetition. You see how well you do; you try to do better than you did before. This we can call *self-monitoring*. You create a little suspense for yourself each time you practice. You think: will this be my "personal best" for doing this?

The third thing to do is to somehow make practicing fun for yourself. You do this largely by talking to yourself in a certain way. Suppose that when you are practicing, you are saying to yourself, "This is so boring, doing the same thing over and over. When will I be done with this, so that I can do something fun? Why do they make me do such boring stuff?" and so forth. Practice won't be fun, and you probably won't be able to get yourself to do very much of it. On the other hand, suppose that you are saying, "Here I go with some more good practices. I'm doing it well! As I do it more, it feels easier and easier! Yay! I did it better than before! Wow, how did I do that? I'm getting able to practice longer and longer! Hooray!" And suppose, as you practice shooting basketball shots, you imagine yourself hitting half-court shots, winning games, and being a star. Suppose, as you practice the cello, you imagine that you'll be good enough to have the audience stand and cheer. Suppose, as you practice the moves for a surgical operation, you imagine that you are one of the foremost surgeons people look to for that operation. And suppose you have already convinced yourself that you would feel super-great to achieve the goal you're working toward, and that you would feel great about getting just a little closer to the goal. *Then* doing lots of practices is not boring -- it's exciting and suspenseful and fun. Your job is to figure out how to make practice fun for yourself. Figure out some way of thinking about it that keeps you from being bored with it. You will need to do lots of celebrating your own accomplishments along the way.

You'll enjoy work on math facts, or almost anything else, if you can also get good at an important skill: doing something fast without getting unpleasantly stressed. If you time yourself at a batch of math facts and say to yourself, "Oh no, oh my gosh, I need to go faster, I can't handle this," and you get yourself anxious and flustered, you won't have fun doing it. If you just relax while you're going faster and faster, it will be fun to watch yourself pick up speed.

Who chooses what you say to yourself and what you imagine while you are practicing? You do! You have some control over whether you will enjoy something or find it boring. Don't think of yourself as a victim. Don't think, "Poor me, I have to do boring things." Think, "If I can use the right mental moves, I can not only learn to get really skilled at this; I can enjoy it, as well!"

Here's another tip for enjoyment. Try to give yourself challenges that are just hard enough, but not too hard. Hopefully you can get, from this book and this experience, how to move to harder challenges when things get too easy, and how, when things get too hard, to move down on the scale of difficulty and work your way back up again.

Let's summarize what this chapter has said. To really get skilled at something, you have to: 1) get the repetition-tolerance that it takes to practice the same things over and over many times, 2) keep monitoring how well you do, and keep trying to do better, and 3) figure out how to make working toward the goal fun and pleasant, not boring or stressful for you. You make work fun and pleasant by celebrating each little step toward the goal, working at the right level of difficulty, imagining success at the goal, and believing that achieving the goal is very worthwhile and will help to make you happy.

Chapter 3: It's Important to See How Big the Numbers Are

When people practice math facts, they most often do it with squiggles that symbolize numbers – squiggles like 9 and 2 and 36 and so forth. But particularly at the beginning of your practicing, it's good to SEE how big the numbers are that you are dealing with.

There's nothing about 9+9 that *looks* like you're dealing with bigger numbers than 2+2. You may be thinking, "I already know that nine is bigger than two." But when you're learning the math facts, the memories will stick in your mind better when you're looking at something that lets you SEE how big the numbers are that you're dealing with.

In this book we're going to use the words "rows" and "columns" a lot. A row goes from left to right on the page, and a column goes up and down.

```
*  *  *  ←This is a row.
*  *  *
*  *  *
↑
```
This is a column.

One way of making a picture of an addition fact like 2+2 is just to get or draw two of something, and then get or draw two more. We picture 2+2 by drawing two rows of asterisks with two in each row, like this:

```
*  *
+
*  *
```

Chapter 3: It's Important to See How Big the Numbers Are

We can picture 9+9 like this:

* * * * * * * * *
\+
* * * * * * * * *

We can see immediately that we're dealing with bigger numbers. But when we have 9 asterisks in a row, we have to count them to know exactly how many there are, and it's easy to lose track while counting, and if you count rows of asterisks like this over and over, it can get very tedious.

There are lots of other ways to make pictures of numbers. One way that people use a lot is the number line. The number line below is a way of visualizing that 6+3=9. The 3 comes in by noticing that if we start at 6 and make 3 jumps to the right (jumping first to 7, second to 8, and third to 9), we end up at 9.

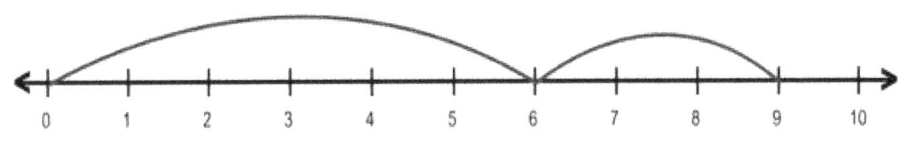

Here's another way of seeing 6 plus 3 equals 9, in a picture of a domino. There are 6 dots in the top panel, and 3 in the bottom, and if we count them all, we get 9.

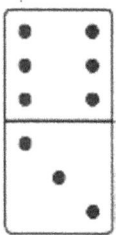

When we make number lines, we don't even have to draw lines. We can make "number lines without the lines" by just writing numbers in order, starting and ending anywhere we choose, like this:

1 2 3 4 5 6 7 8 9 10

(It's as though the numbers "got in line.") To see that 6 + 3 = 9, just put your finger on six, jump three numbers to the right, and notice that you land on 9.

Suppose that we wanted to continue our "number line without a line," but we ran out of space. We could go one row down and keep going.

1   2   3   4   5   6   7   8   9 10
11 12 13 14 15 16 17 18 19 20

I'll call this a "broken number line." You can use it for adding, just as you would an unbroken number line. For example, if you want to add 9+3, you start on the 9, and make the first jump to 10, the second to 11, and the third jump landing on 12. So 9+3=12.

Chapter 3: It's Important to See How Big the Numbers Are

Let's use this number line to add 10+3. We start at 10. We make one jump to 11, the second to 12, and the third to land on 13. So 10+3=13. Do you notice that the 13 is right under the 3 on the top row, and 3 is what we were adding? That isn't just a coincidence, because we are adding something to 10, and we broke the number line right after 10.

Please add 10+5. Put your finger on 10, and make 5 jumps. One jump puts you on 11, 2 puts you on 12, 3 puts you on 13, 4 puts you on 14, and 5 puts you on 15. The 15 is right under the 5 on the top row, and 5 is what we were adding to 10.

Broken number lines are a great way to see addition facts. When we do 10+5, we see 10 numbers in the first row. We make 5 jumps forward along the number line, so that there are now 5 more numbers. But it isn't so hard to count the 5 jumps, because the numbers on the first line do the counting for us. After 5 jumps, we're going to land on a number right under the number 5.

We're going to make great use of broken number lines. First, though, we want to figure out which facts we really need to learn.

Chapter 4: Ideas That Let Us Memorize Fewer Addition Facts

Order doesn't make a difference

Groups of stars or dots or any sort of thing can illustrate addition. Look at these asterisks:

✻ ✻ ✻   ✻ ✻

There are 3 in the group on the left, and 2 in the group on the right, and 5 altogether.

Let's imagine that we started with the group on the left, and then added on the group on the right. We would find that 3 + 2 = 5. But suppose we start with the group on the right, and add on the group that's on the left. This lets us see that 2 + 3 = 5. We are going to end up with 5 asterisks, no matter which group we start with and which we add on.

Another good way to see that order doesn't make a difference is by looking at a picture of a domino.

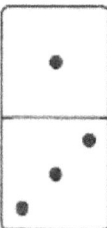

There is one dot on the top square, 3 dots on the bottom square, and 4 altogether. If we start with the top square and add on the bottom, we illustrate that 1+3=4. But if we start with the bottom square and add on the top, we illustrate that 3+1=4. Just looking at the domino, is it easy to see that we have two groups, and they total to four dots, and it doesn't make any difference in what order we look at them?

It's the same with all addition facts. 5 + 4 gives the same answer as 4 + 5. 248 + 379 gives the same answer as 379 + 248.

The fact that order doesn't make a difference when we add is called the commutative law of addition. This law is good news, because it cuts our work down a lot! Once we've learned 9 + 3, we automatically know 3 + 9; we don't have to learn it all over again.

Adding 0

If you add 0 to any number, you get the same number you started with. 5+0=5. 10+0=10. 0+1=1. Makes sense, doesn't it? It makes even more sense with real life situations – for example, you have 5 pencils, and you get no more, or get zero more, you still have 5. On our number line,

0 1 2 3 4 5 6 7 8 9 10

we can start at 5 and take zero jumps to the right. That leaves us at 5, right where we started!

So we don't need to memorize the "0 pluses" or the "plus 0's!"

Adding 1

If you add 1 to any whole number, you land on the next higher number when you count. In other words, adding 1 just gets you to the next number. So, for example, when we count, we go 6, 7, 8, 9 ..., which tells us that 6+1=7, 7+1=8, and 8+1=9.

Here's a number line picture of adding 7+1:

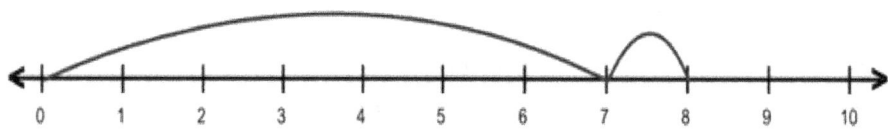

So as long as we know really well how to count, we don't need to memorize the plus 1's or the 1 pluses!

Adding 10

If you add 10 to any number from 0 to 9, you just put a 1 to the left of the number, and you have your answer. For example, to add 10 to 3, we'll just put a 1 to the left of the 3, and we get 13. 10+5=15, 10+9=19, and so forth.

When you add 10+10, you get 2 10s, or 20.

Here's a picture of the 10 pluses with a broken number line.

1 2 3 4 5 6 7 8 9 10

11 12 13 14 15 16 17 18 19 20

This gives us a picture of how 10 plus any one-digit number results in that number with a 1 to the left of it.

Chapter 4: Ideas That Let Us Memorize Fewer Addition Facts

How much memorizing have we now saved?

How many different addition facts are there, using the numbers from 0 to 10? We have 11 choices for the first number, (1 through 10 plus 0) and for each of those, we have 11 choices for the second number. We have 11 x 11 or 121 different possible addition facts.

But what happens if we leave out everything that our four rules keep us from having to memorize? We eliminate all but these 36:

1. 2+2=4

2. 3+2=5
3. 3+3=6

4. 4+2=6
5. 4+3=7
6. 4+4=8

7. 5+2=7
8. 5+3=8
9. 5+4=9
10. 5+5=10

11. 6+2=8
12. 6+3=9
13. 6+4=10
14. 6+5=11
15. 6+6=12

16. 7+2=9
17. 7+3=10
18. 7+4=11
19. 7+5=12
20. 7+6=13
21. 7+7=14

22. 8+2=10
23. 8+3=11
24. 8+4=12
25. 8+5=13
26. 8+6=14
27. 8+7=15
28. 8+8=16

29. 9+2=11
30. 9+3=12
31. 9+4=13
32. 9+5=14
33. 9+6=15
34. 9+7=16
35. 9+8=17
36. 9+9=18

So one of our big goals is to get these 36 addition facts thoroughly memorized!

I recommend that you use the 36 addition facts printed above to see how fast you can go when the answers are printed for you. First, time yourself just saying the answers. One easy way to get the number of facts per minute is just to keep going for exactly a minute, starting over at the beginning if you reach the end. If, for example, you do all 36 and get through number 30 the second time around, you have done 36+30 or 66 per minute. Second, time yourself saying the questions and answers: "Two plus two, four. Three plus two, five. Three plus three, six." And so forth. I recommend leaving out the word "equals," to save time. Again, see how many you can do per minute. However fast you can get your mouth to move, to say these, is the speed you eventually want to shoot for when answering the questions in random order.

The rest of this book has lots of practices and drills. I recommend doing them without rushing yourself or timing yourself until you feel that you can do them completely accurately, and very easily -- so easily that you need to start pushing yourself toward greater speed so that you won't be bored. Then time yourself for any given exercise and see if you can do it faster and faster. But even while you are doing time trials, see if you can relax. Don't fret. Going quickly without making yourself worried and anxious is a great skill to cultivate!

Chapter 5: Practicing Adding With Ordinary Number Lines

Before we start using broken number lines, practice some adding with regular number lines. Here's a picture of a number line from 0 to 20. You can figure out the answer to any of the basic addition facts using this number line.

Suppose you want to know 5+4. You can start at the 5, and jump 4 steps to the right. You say 1, 2, 3, 4 as your finger goes to 6, 7, 8, and 9. So you end up at 9, and that's the answer.

When you're figuring out addition facts using the number line, remember not to count the number you start on. So when you're doing 5 plus 4, you count 1 when you go to 6. You don't count 1 on the 5, because 5 is 0 steps from 5, not 1 step.

Please practice figuring out addition facts using the number line. How about 4+6? Start at the 4 and jump 6 units (or steps) to the right. Count from 1 to 6, counting 1 each time you make a jump. What did you get?

How about 3+5? Start at the 3 and jump 5 units to the right. What did you get? Now how about 5+3. Please start at 5 and make 3 jumps to the right, even if you already know what the answer will be. Hopefully you just demonstrated the "order doesn't make a difference" rule for addition.

How about 8+7? Start at the 8 and jump 7 units to the right.

How about 9+8? Start at the 9 and move 8 units to the right.

You can make a number line any time you want to figure out a basic addition (or subtraction) fact that you can't remember. You don't need to draw a line. You can just write the numbers:

0 1 2 3 4 5 6 7 8 9 10 11 12 13 14 15 16 17 18 19 20

Please practice using this "number line without the line" to figure out, or demonstrate, some math facts.

How about 9+4. Start at 9 and move 4 units to the right.

Now, if a tutor and a student are working together, the tutor can give out a few of our 36 addition facts listed earlier, and let the student use the number line to tell the answers. You don't have to do this a long time or get very fast at it. But it's great to have some experience actually moving your finger or the eraser end of a pencil to have the experience of adding by jumping along the number line.

Chapter 6: Adding Using Broken Number Lines

We have just talked about adding using number lines. If we want, we can break our number lines into pieces, and arrange them in more than one row on the page. We still get the same answers. This is very much like the words on this page. We don't have room to keep going in one long line of words, so we break the line and start back under the previous one. We read from left to right, until we get to the end of the line, and then we go down.

Please look at this broken number line:

1	2	3	4	5	6
7	8	9	10	11	12

Let's add 6+3 using this number line. We start at the 6. 1 jump forward lands us on 7, 2 jumps on 8, and 3 jumps on 9. So 6 + 3 = 9.

We broke the number line after 6. The number we added to 6 was 3. The answer we landed on was right under the 3 in the top row. Was that a coincidence? No, it isn't a coincidence.

Let's add 1 to 6. That lands us on 7, and it's under the 1. If we add 2 to 6, we land on 8, which is under the 2. Adding 3 to 6 we land on 9, which is under the 3. Under the 4 we find the answer to 6+4. Under the 5 we find the answer to 6+5. Under the 6 we find the answer to 6+6. It's not a coincidence that we find the number right under the number we are adding to 6!

With this broken number line, we don't have to be so careful counting the number of jumps up from 6. The first line does the counting for us, doesn't it?

But the broken number line above is especially convenient only when one of the numbers we're adding is 6. Let's do 5+3 on the broken number line above. We would start at 5 and make 3 jumps farther along.

Learning the Math Facts

We'd end up at 8, if we count our jumps accurately, and that's the right answer. But 8 isn't under the 3. We can't use the "6 plus" line very conveniently when we're adding various numbers to 5. But how about if we broke the number line right after the 5? Let's look at the number line that's broken after 5:

1	2	3	4	5
6	7	8	9	10

Now let's do 5+3. We start at 5; one jump is to 6; 2 jumps is to 7; 3 jumps is to 8. And 8 is right underneath the 3 in the first row! When we break at 5, the numbers on the top help us count how many jumps up from 5 we've made along the number line.

So the line broken at 6 is really convenient for adding numbers to 6. The line broken at 5 is really convenient for adding numbers to 5!

If you look at the broken number line above, you can see that 5+1=6 (and the answer is under the 1); 5+2=7 (that 7 is right under the 2); 5+3=8 (which is under the 3); 5+4=9 (the 9 is right under the 4) and 5+5=10 (the 10 is under the 5)!

We have a pattern going here! A number line broken after 2 is good for adding numbers to 2; a number line broken after 3 is good for adding to 3; breaking after 4 is good for adding to 4; and so on.

On the next page, let's make broken number lines starting at 2 and going up to 9. If you get the hang of using the broken number lines, you can use this page to see a number line representation of all the 36 addition facts we listed earlier, and the plus 1's as a bonus.

Chapter 6: Adding Using Broken Number Lines

Broken number lines for addition facts

2 pluses
1   2
3   4

3 pluses
1   2   3
4   5   6

4 pluses
1   2   3   4
5   6   7   8

5 pluses
1   2   3   4   5
6   7   8   9   10

6 pluses
1   2   3   4   5   6
7   8   9   10   11   12

7 pluses
1   2   3   4   5   6   7
8   9   10   11   12   13   14

8 pluses
1   2   3   4   5   6   7   8
9   10   11   12   13   14   15   16

9 pluses
1   2   3   4   5   6   7   8   9
10   11   12   13   14   15   16   17   18

Why are there only two addition facts illustrated for the plus 2's? Why does the number line broken at 2 only go up to 2+2? Where do we find facts like 2+3, 2+4, and so forth? They're on the page, if you can find them! 2+3 is the same as 3+2, and you find that on the "3 pluses" line. 2+4 is the same as 4+2, and you find that on the "4 pluses" broken line. All the facts you need are there, as long as you use the "order doesn't make a difference" rule. (This rule is also known as the commutative law of addition!) We avoid duplicating facts if we stop at the "double," where the number is added to itself. You'll notice that the 4 pluses go up to 4+4, the 5 pluses up to 5+5, and so on.

We can drill on addition facts, using the previous page as an aid. Suppose one person is a tutor and a second person is a student. The tutor might say, "Can you please go to the broken line for the plus 4's, and say the four "4 plus" addition facts in order?"

The student would find the line that looks like this:

4 pluses
1   2   3   4
5   6   7   8

And the student would say: "4+1=5. 4+2=6. 4+3=7. 4+4=8."

Then, the tutor might say, "Now please say those 4 pluses in random order. Just skip around, and say those facts in no particular order."

The student would look at the broken number line to make it easier, and would say things like this: "4+3=7. 4+1=5. 4+4=8. 4+3=7. 4+2=6. 4+1=5. 4+2=6." The tutor checks to make sure each fact is correct, and celebrates.

Chapter 6: Adding Using Broken Number Lines

The student can also do this sort of drill alone. Suppose you want to drill on the 8 pluses.

1	2	3	4	5	6	7	8
9	10	11	12	13	14	15	16

You would first take one jump higher than 8, and see the 9 right under the 1. You say to yourself, "8+1=9." If you take 2 jumps up from 8, you land on the 10, right under the 2, and you say to yourself, "8+2=10." Then you continue in order, saying, "8+3=11; 8+4=12; 8+5=13; 8+6=14; 8+7=15; 8+8=16." You can do this lots of times.

By the way, there is something interesting about the plus 8's. As you do them, you may notice that the second digit in the sum is two less than the number you're adding to 8. For example, when adding 8+5, we get 13; the 3 is two less than the 5. When adding 8+6, we get 14; the 4 is two less than the 6. This works because adding 8 is the same as adding 10 – 2. If we add 10 and take away 2, that's the same as adding 8!

Back to drilling with the 8 pluses. After you've gone in order, you can go in random order. You can say to yourself (or better still, you can say aloud) something like: "8+5=13. 8+8=16. 8+3=11. 8+2=10. 8+4=12. 8+8=16. 8+7=15." And so forth, for long enough to give a workout to your repetition-tolerance muscles!

The next big step is to look away from the page and see if you can do the facts in order without looking. If you need to, you can always look back at the page.

The next big step is to look away from the page and see if you can do the facts in random order without looking. Again, feel free to look back at the page if you need to.

When you get to the 9 pluses, there's something interesting that is very much like what we noticed with the 8 pluses, only easier. You see that the last digit in the answer is 1 less than the number added to 9.

9 pluses

1	2	3	4	5	6	7	8	9
10	11	12	13	14	15	16	17	18

So 9+5=14, and the 4 in 14 is one less than 5. 9+6=15, and the 5 in 15 is one less than the 6 we added to 9. So to add any number to 9, you can add 10 and subtract 1.

Here's another way to drill when two people are working together. The first, in the role of the tutor, calls out a question and the other says the answer. They start out focusing on accuracy and then gradually get faster and faster. They drill on one set of the facts at a time. For example, they might look at this part of the page

7 pluses

1	2	3	4	5	6	7
8	9	10	11	12	13	14

And the tutor might say: 7+6. The student says 13. The tutor says 7+3. The student says 10. The tutor says 7+5. The student says 12. And they keep going for a long time. The student looks at the broken number line as much as is desired. The student relies on the broken number line enough so that this drill can go on quickly and easily. Whenever the student is up for more challenge, the student tries to answer the questions without looking at the broken number line.

Chapter 6: Adding Using Broken Number Lines

Adding a whole row with broken number lines

Are you ready to think about the broken number lines in a new way? We've been thinking of this broken line as representing the "5 pluses": numbers added to 5. We start with 5 and add the other number to 5.

1   2   3   4   5
6   7   8   9   10

But here's the new idea: we can also think about this broken number line as representing the "plus 5s": starting with a number and adding 5 to it! Of course, we'll get the same thing as if we started with 5 and added the number to 5. But I want you to be able to think of the broken number line above as "plus 5s" as well as "5 pluses."

Let's start with 4 on the broken number line above. Please take 5 jumps in the direction of greater numbers. One jump lands on 5, two lands on 6, three jumps lands on 7, four lands on 8, and the fifth jump lands on 9, our answer for 4+5. Hmm. We started at 4, and when we added 5, we ended up directly beneath the 4, one row down. And that wasn't a coincidence!

Please take the same broken number line and start with 2, and add 5 by making 5 jumps. Do you land on 7, right beneath the 2? When we add 5 to 3, we land on the 8, right beneath the 3. And so forth.

Why does adding 5 to any number put us on the next row down, right under the number? Because there are 5 in each row. Therefore, adding 5 moves us exactly one row down from wherever we started!

What's the difference between this and what we were doing before? Before, we were always starting at the number at the end of the first row, and adding numbers to it. For example, with 5+3, we started at 5, and noticed that 3 jumps greater was under the 3. Now we can start anywhere in the first row, and add to it the number in the row, by going

Learning the Math Facts

one row down. We can use our broken number line to think about 3+5, whereas before we were using it to think of 5+3.

Let's go through the same reasoning with another broken number line. Let's use the line that's broken after 4. We'll now use it to add 4 to something else.

| 1 | 2 | 3 | 4 |
| 5 | 6 | 7 | 8 |

How about starting at 1, and counting 4 jumps in the direction of greater numbers. We land on 5, right beneath the 4. So we've represented that 1+4 is 5. Let's start on 3, and count 4 jumps more. We land on 7, right beneat the 3, and we've demonstrated that 3+4 is 7.

Why does going down exactly one row add 4 this time, when it added 5 before? Because now there are 4 in each row! We broke this number line at 4 rather than at 5.

Does that make sense? If it does, please go back to the page with all the broken number lines on it. Look, for example, at the 9 pluses, and think of them as the Plus 9's. Start with 1, and look one row under it, and say 1+9=10. Go to 2, look one row under it, and say 2+9=11. Keep going: 3+9=12; 4+9=13, and so forth, in order. Now say plus 9's in random order, and then say the answers with someone giving them out to you in random order.

If two people are working together, let the tutor click a tally counter for each fact, and just keep going long enough to stretch your repetition-tolerance some. Soon, hopefully, you will become able to go very fast, in random order, with each of the broken number lines. It's OK to keep using the broken number lines to help you with the answers. You want them to come out of your mouth (and go through your brain) very fast and very many times.

On the next page I'll repeat the broken number lines. Only now we'll label them for example 5 pluses (or plus 5s), since now we can think of them in either way.

The Broken Number Line Page for Addition

2 pluses or plus 2s
1   2
3   4

3 pluses or plus 3s
1   2   3
4   5   6

4 pluses or plus 4s
1   2   3   4
5   6   7   8

5 pluses or plus 5s
1   2   3   4   5
6   7   8   9   10

6 pluses or plus 6s
1   2   3   4   5   6
7   8   9   10   11   12

7 pluses or plus 7s
1   2   3   4   5   6   7
8   9   10   11   12   13   14

8 pluses or plus 8s
1   2   3   4   5   6   7   8
9   10   11   12   13   14   15   16

9 pluses or plus 9s
1   2   3   4   5   6   7   8   9
10   11   12   13   14   15   16   17   18

Chapter 7: Ideas for Reducing Memorization in Subtraction

Subtraction is the opposite, (or inverse) of addition

Taking away is the opposite of adding on. If I have 3 apples and get 2 more, I have 5; if someone takes away 2 apples, I'm back at 3. Subtracting 2 "undoes" what adding 2 did. For that reason, if we know that 3+2 = 5, then we don't have to start all over again to memorize separately the fact that 5-2=3.

Let's think about this using the number line.

1 2 3 4 5 6 7 8 9 10

If we start at 3, and make 2 jumps to the right, we land on 5. If we start at 5 and make 2 jumps to the left, we land back at 3. (Addition means jumping to the right on the number line, and subtraction means jumping to the left.)

And let's picture the same thing using a domino.

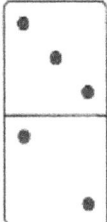

We see that starting with the 3 dots on top, and adding 2 more dots on the bottom, yields 5 dots altogether. But the same picture tells us that if we start out looking at all 5 dots, and then cover up the 2 on the bottom, we have 3 left. We see in another way that 3+2=5 and 5-2=3 are sort of different ways of saying the same thing. We call them facts in the same "fact family." When you have memorized one, it should not be much work to memorize the other.

If we combine this idea with the "order doesn't make a difference" rule for addition, we come up with 4 members of any family where the two numbers are different. For the 3+2 family, we have:

3+2=5
2+3=5
5-2=3
5-3=2.

If the two numbers being added are the same, the fact family only has two members. For example,

2+2=4
4-2=2.

You can use fact families to cut down greatly on the amount of memorizing you do to get good at subtraction, once you are good at addition.

Subtracting 0, and subtracting a number from itself

If you subtract 0 from any number, you wind up with the same number. For example, 3-0=3.

If you subtract any number from itself, you wind up with 0. For example, 3-3=0.

Chapter 7: Ideas for Reducing Memorization in Subtraction

Subtracting 1, and subtracting the number just before a number

If you subtract 1 from any counting number, you get the number just before it. For example, 5-1=4.

If you subtract from any counting number the number just before it, you get 1. For example, 5-4=1.

Subtracting 10 from a number in the range from 11 to 19

To subtract 10 from a number from 11 to 19, you just knock off the 1 that is in the ten's place. For example, 12-10=2. 15-10=5. 14-10=4.

Subtracting the number in the ones' place from a number from 11 to 19

If you have a number in the range from 11 to 19 and subtract the number in the ones' place, you get 10. For example: for 15, 5 is the number in the ones' place. 15-5=10. 16-6=10, 17-7=10, and so forth.

Practice using these rules

Let's practice some of the subtraction facts that you don't have to memorize if you understand the rules we've just mentioned.

1. 6-0=
2. 9-9=
3. 7-1=
4. 8-7=
5. 13-10=

6. 12-2=
7. 8-0=
8. 5-5=
9. 5-1=
10. 9-8=

11. 14-10=
12. 16-6=

Chapter 8: Subtracting Using Ordinary Number Lines

Here's a picture of an ordinary number line.

Subtracting, as we mentioned in the previous chapter, is the opposite of addition. If we add 6 + 2, we start at the 6 and go 2 jumps to the right, landing on the 8. If we subtract, 8-2, we start at the 8 and go 2 jumps to the left. We land on the 6.

You might do a little practice at subtracting, using the number line. How about 9-1? How about 11-2? How about 7-3? Did you land on 8, 9, and 4 when you did those?

Subtracting using the ordinary number line involves some careful counting when the numbers are a little bigger. For example, please do 15-9 on the number line. If you landed on 6, you counted your jumps carefully. But it was a bit tedious, wasn't it?

As was the case before with addition, we can do subtraction of whole numbers just fine without bothering to draw a line, but just using a row of numbers. How about using this "number line" to do a bit of subtraction.

0 1 2 3 4 5 6 7 8 9 10 11 12 13 14 15 16 17 18 19 20

So to do 13-3, we start at 13 and take 3 jumps to the left, landing on the 10. It's not any harder when we don't bother to draw the line, is it?

Please do a little practice with subtracting using the number line. If a tutor is working with a student, please let the tutor give some subtraction problems and let the student find the answer by jumping to the left along the number line. Student, if you already know the answers, please do a little jumping along the number line anyway, just to have the experience of moving your finger to subtract.

Chapter 9 : Subtracting Using Broken Number Lines

Let's look at the broken number line we used when we thought about the 5 pluses and the plus 5's:

```
1   2   3   4   5
6   7   8   9   10
```

When we think about subtraction using this broken number line, we start with a number in the bottom row. Let's start with 6. If we make 1 jump toward smaller numbers, we land on 5. So we have illustrated that 6-1=5. (And the 6 is right under the 1.) If we start on 7 and make 2 jumps toward smaller, we land on 5. So we've illustrated that 7-2=5. (And the 7 is right under the 2.) And so forth, in order: 8-3=5, 9-4=5, 10-5=5. We can call these the "make 5" subtraction facts. Please say them in order: 6-1=5; 7-2=5; 8-3=5; 9-4=5; 10-5=5.

The next step is to say the "make 5" subtraction facts in random order. For example: 9-4=5; 7-2=5; 10-5=5; 6-1=5, and so forth. Practice this a lot.

The next step is to look away from the page and say the "make 5" subtraction facts in order. Look back at the page only if you need to.

The next step is to look away from the page and say the "make 5" subtraction facts in random order. Look back at the page if you need to.

Learning the Math Facts

We could have started with the 2s.

1   2
3   4

The "make 2" math facts in order are 3-1=2, and 4-2=2.

We can do the 3s.

1   2   3
4   5   6

The "make 3" math facts in order are 4-1=3, 5-2=3, 6-3=3.

Now I'm going to repeat the page of broken number lines again, and you can practice the make 2s through the make 9s with it.

Chapter 9 : Subtracting Using Broken Number Lines

2 pluses, plus 2s, or make 2s
1   2
3   4

3 pluses, plus 2s, or make 2s
1   2   3
4   5   6

4 pluses, plus 4s, or make 4s
1   2   3   4
5   6   7   8

5 pluses, plus 5s, or make 5s
1   2   3   4   5
6   7   8   9   10

6 pluses, plus 6s, or make 6s
1   2   3   4   5   6
7   8   9   10 11 12

7 pluses, plus 7s, or make 7s
1   2   3   4   5   6   7
8   9   10 11 12 13 14

8 pluses, plus 8s, or make 8s
1   2   3   4   5   6   7   8
9   10 11 12 13 14 15 16

9 pluses, plus 9s, or make 9s
1   2   3   4   5   6   7   8   9
10 11 12 13 14 15 16 17 18

Now let's go back to the number line broken at 5.

Remember that there were two ways of thinking about addition using our broken number lines, so that the 5 line could be 5 pluses or plus 5s? There are also two ways of thinking about subtraction. Are you ready for another new way of thinking?

| 1 | 2 | 3 | 4 | 5 |
| 6 | 7 | 8 | 9 | 10 |

The second way of thinking about subtraction with this broken number line is the "minus 5s." Let's say we start at 6 and subtract 5. With 5 in each row, 5 jumps lower means moving exactly 1 row up. Try it and see – start with 6 and go backwards 5 jumps. You land one row higher, at the 1. We've represented that 6-5=1. Now let's do 7-5 on the broken number line. Please count backwards 5 jumps from 7, and you see that we land one row higher, right over the 7, on the 2. How about 8-5? We take our 5 jumps backward and land on the 3.

Whenever we subtract 5 from any number in the second row, the answer is the number right above it in the first row. This is true because we broke the number line at 5, so that there are 5 numbers in a row.

So an important step is to look at the broken number line and say the minus 5s in order: 6-5=1, 7-5=2, 8-5=3, 9-5=4, 10-5=5.

The next step, as you may guess, is to say the minus 5s in random order, looking at the broken number line.

The next step is to say the minus 5s in order, not looking at the page, but looking back if you need to.

The next step is to say the minus 5s in random order, not looking at the page unless you have to.

And finally, the next step is to do this sort of subtraction fact with the rest of the broken number lines! I'm repeating this page for the 4th time, for your convenience.

You will want to use this page a lot. It takes some mental work to look at a line broken, say at 6, and realize that you can use this to represent adding number to 6, adding 6 to numbers, subtracting numbers to make 6, and subtracting 6 from numbers. Keep practicing with each of these 4 ways of thinking until you really understand them. When you feel shaky, figure out some of the facts by actually counting forward or backward along the number line.

Broken number line page for addition and subtraction

2 pluses, plus 2s, make 2s, or minus 2s
1 2
3 4

3 pluses, plus 3s, make 3s, or minus 3s
1 2 3
4 5 6

4 pluses, plus 4s, make 4s, or minus 4s
1 2 3 4
5 6 7 8

5 pluses, plus 5s, make 5s, or minus 5s
1 2 3 4 5
6 7 8 9 10

6 pluses, plus 6s, make 6s, or minus 6s
1 2 3 4 5 6
7 8 9 10 11 12

7 pluses, plus 7s, make 7s, or minus 7s
1 2 3 4 5 6 7
8 9 10 11 12 13 14

8 pluses, plus 8s, make 8s, or minus 8s
1 2 3 4 5 6 7 8
9 10 11 12 13 14 15 16

9 pluses, plus 9s, make 9s, or minus 9s
1 2 3 4 5 6 7 8 9
10 11 12 13 14 15 16 17 18

Chapter 10: Fact Families, and dominoes to Show Them

We've now come far enough to see that with our broken number lines, each number on the bottom row (except for the last one) can remind us of 4 math facts. Let's look at our 3 plus number line, and start with the 4 on the bottom row.

1   2   3
4   5   6

We landed here with 3+1. We also landed here with 1+3. If we do 4-1, we "make 3." And if we do 4-3, a "minus 3," we land on 1. So there are 4 facts associated with this:

3+1=4 (the "3 plus")
1+3=4 (the "plus 3")
4-1=3 (the "make 3")
4-3=1. (the "minus 3")

How about the 5, on the same number line?

1   2   3
4   **5**   6

This reminds us that:
3+2=5 (the 3 plus)
2+3=5 (the plus 3)
5-2=3 (the make 3)
and 5-3=2 (the minus 3).

Learning the Math Facts

The "3 and 2" family is another "fact family" with 4 members. It's worthwhile to take your finger and do each of these on the number line, even though you may already know the facts. Start at the 3 and go 2 forward to land on 5; start at 2 and go 3 forward to land on 5; start at 5 and go 2 backward to land on 3; start at 5 and go 3 backward to land on 2.

When we get to the 6 on the same broken number line, we get
3+3=6 (the 3 plus)
3+3=6 (the plus 3)
6-3=3 (the make 3)
And 6-3=3 (the minus 3).

1	2	3
4	5	**<u>6</u>**

But the first two and the last two of these are the same fact. So there are only 2 members of this fact family. This is the same with all the "doubles" like 4+4, 5+5, and so forth.

If you can use the broken number lines to say all the fact families, that's great. It's worth practicing a lot.

The addition and subtraction facts are so important that it's good to practice seeing them in at least one more way than the broken number lines. Are you ready for a new way of visualizing addition and subtraction facts? Here we go, with dominoes!

If you've used "double nine" dominoes for playing games, you may be able to recognize right away how many dots are in a certain square. If you're not familiar with dominoes, you may need to count

Chapter 10: Fact Families, and dominoes to Show Them

them a few times before you can recognize the number of dots right away.

For the 2 pluses, for example, instead of this broken number line:

1   2
3   4

we can look at these dominoes.

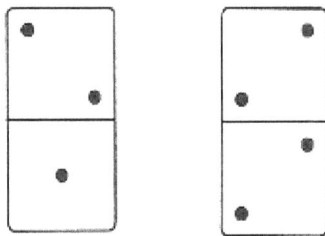

The domino on the left has 2 dots on the top square and one on the bottom, and 3 altogether. So this domino shows us that 2+1=3. And if we start with the bottom square, we see that 1+2=3. If we start with all 3 dots on the same domino, and cover up the 2 dots on the top square with our thumb, we demonstrate that 3-2=1. If we start with 3 and cover up the 1 dot on the bottom square with our thumb, this demonstrates that 3-1=2.

So the entire fact family for the domino on the left is: 2+1=3; 1+2=3; 3-2=1; 3-1=2.

The domino on the right is a double, so it has a fact family with two members: 2+2=4, and 4-2=2.

I'll present below pictures of dominoes for you to use in saying fact families. Look at each domino and say each member of the fact family that goes with that domino. This gives you more practice in addition and subtraction facts, and another way of seeing a picture of them in your mind.

Below are the dominoes for the three pluses:

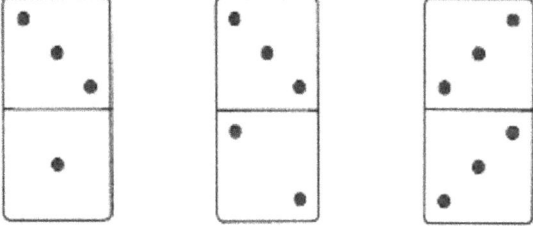

Below are the dominoes for the 4 pluses:

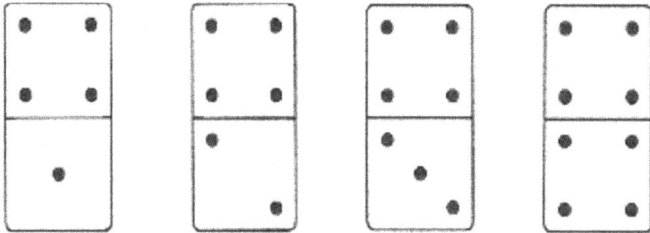

Below are the dominoes for the 5 pluses:

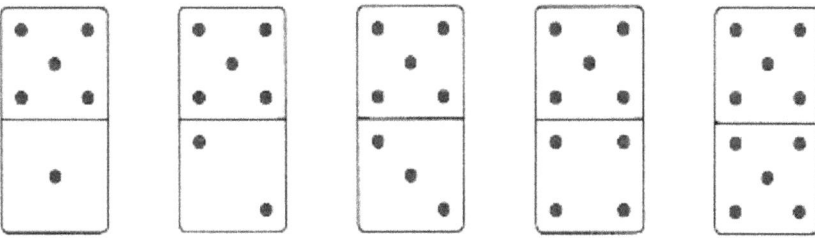

Below are the dominoes for the 6 pluses:

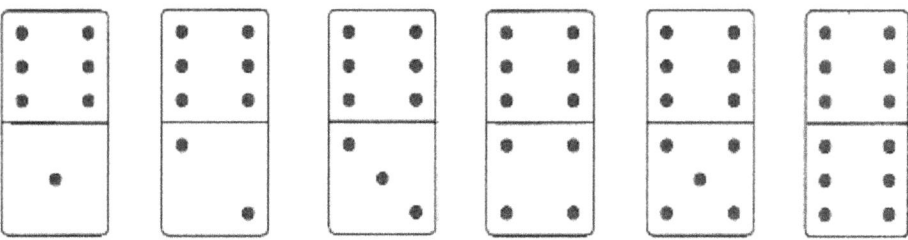

Below are the dominoes for the 7 pluses:

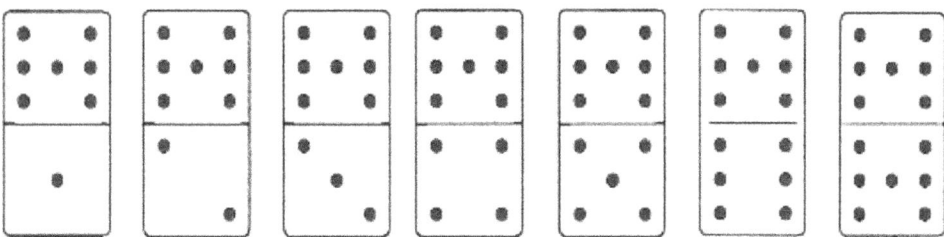

Below are the dominoes for the 8 pluses:

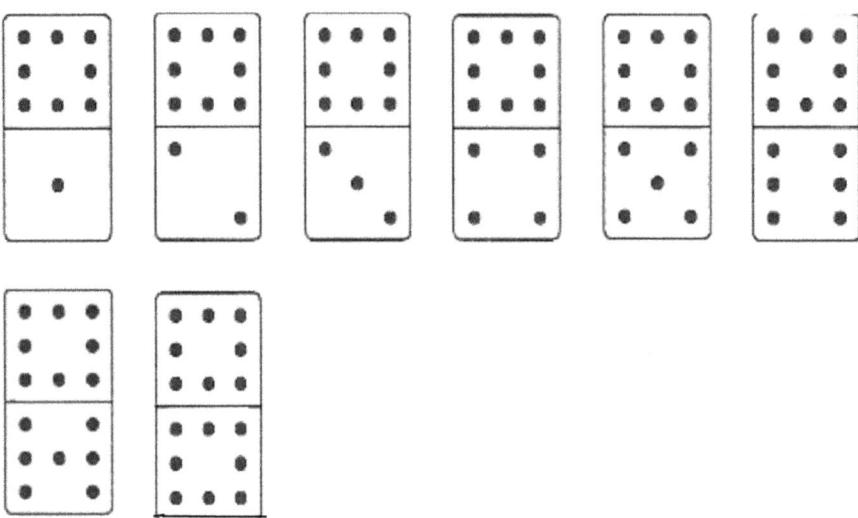

And below are the dominoes for the 9 pluses:

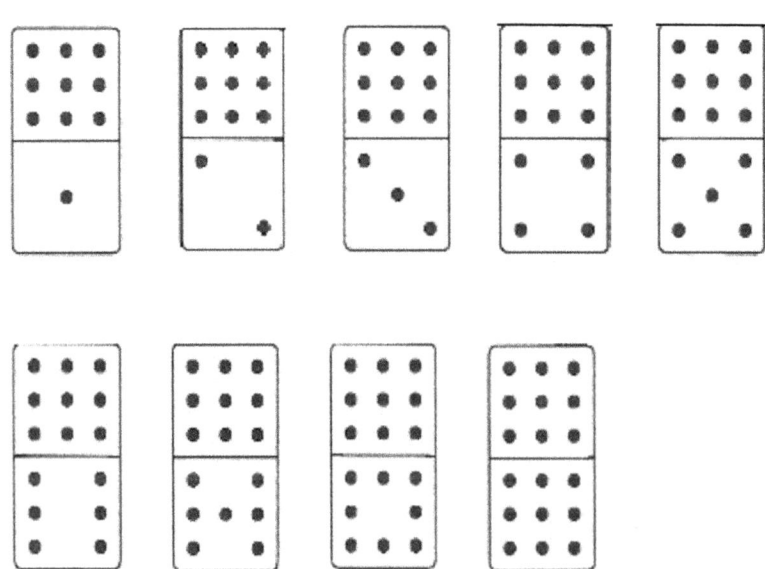

Chapter 10: Fact Families, and dominoes to Show Them

I recommend practicing in this way with the dominoes:

1. For any given set (the 2s, the 3s, etc. up through the 9s) look at the dominoes in order and say the fact families for each of them. Keep doing that with just that set, until you can say the fact families for the dominoes in that set, very quickly.

2. Do the same thing with the other sets, until you have done them all.

3. Practice saying the fact families for all the sets of dominoes, in order, from start to finish, as fast as you can. Keep going until you can do this about as fast as you can get the words out of your mouth.

After you've done a lot of practicing with the dominoes, please go back to one of the pages of broken number lines. You can now practice saying addition and subtraction facts, at random, looking at the various number lines. Or if you want, you can go back and drill on one set, just as you did before. Don't be afraid of repetition, because it's what leads to success with math facts.

Chapter 11: Optional: One More Way of Visualizing Addition and Subtraction

This is an optional chapter. I include it because you will see the table below in lots of books, more often than you'll see the sorts of broken number lines we used earlier.

The addition table below is another way of visualizing addition and subtraction, that is similar to the broken number lines we've used.

0	1	2	**3**	4	5	6	7	8	9	10
1	2	3	**4**	5	6	7	8	9	10	11
2	3	4	**5**	6	7	8	9	10	11	12
3	4	5	**6**	7	8	9	10	11	12	13
4	**5**	**6**	**7**	8	9	10	11	12	13	14
5	6	7	8	9	10	11	12	13	14	15
6	7	8	9	10	11	12	13	14	15	16
7	8	9	10	11	12	13	14	15	16	17
8	9	10	11	12	13	14	15	16	17	18
9	10	11	12	13	14	15	16	17	18	19
10	11	12	13	14	15	16	17	18	19	20

Suppose we want to know what 4+3 is, (and we don't already have it memorized). Look at the row that starts with 4. It goes 4, 5, 6, 7, 8, and so forth. This is a number line, isn't it? You could start with 4 and count 3 jumps to the right, and get the answer, 7. But you don't really need to count the jumps, because the top row (the one that starts 0, 1, 2, 3…) does it for you. So you can look in row starting with 4, in the column directly under the 3 in the first row, and get the answer.

Chapter 11: Optional: One More Way of Visualizing Addition and Subtraction

As a more general rule: to find the sum of any two numbers, you look where the row starting with one of them crosses the column starting with the other one.

One of the disadvantages of using this table at the beginning of your learning math facts is that it makes the job look a lot bigger than it is. There are 121 answers to addition facts in this table. It shows 3+4 separately from 4+3, for example, and doesn't take advantage of the "order makes a difference" rule; it shows the plus 0's. Another disadvantage is that when we find, for example, 3+4, where, exactly, are the 7 things? It's not so obvious as with the broken number lines we used earlier. But by now, we're into drilling on all possible facts, and more repetition is better than less, and it may help you to see things in more than one way. We can drill with this table in various different ways. Here's the table again:

0	1	2	3	4	5	6	7	8	9	10
1	2	3	4	5	6	7	8	9	10	11
2	3	4	5	6	7	8	9	10	11	12
3	4	5	6	7	8	9	10	11	12	13
4	5	6	7	8	9	10	11	12	13	14
5	6	7	8	9	10	11	12	13	14	15
6	7	8	9	10	11	12	13	14	15	16
7	8	9	10	11	12	13	14	15	16	17
8	9	10	11	12	13	14	15	16	17	18
9	10	11	12	13	14	15	16	17	18	19
10	11	12	13	14	15	16	17	18	19	20

And here are some things to do with it:

1. Looking at the table, say addition facts in order. The top row is the "zero row," since it starts with zero. It shows that: "0+0=0; 0+1=1; 0+2=2; 0+3=3;" and so forth. The next row is the "1 row," since it starts with 1. It shows that "1+0=1; 1+1=2; 1+2=3; 1+3=4;" and so forth. For

the "2 row," you start out by saying "2+0=2; 2+1=3; 2+2=4; and so forth." If you want to concentrate on some particular row, such as the 7 pluses or 8 pluses, you can of course say the addition facts in order for any rows you want without having to go through all 121 of them.

2. Rather than just saying the addition facts in order, you can for any row say the fact families in order. For example, for the row beginning with 8, you can say "8+0=8; 0+8=8; 8-0=8; 8-8=0; 8+1=9; 1+8=9; 9-1=8; 9-8=1;" and so forth.

3. For any row, you can say either the addition facts or the fact families in random order. Looking at row 8, you can say, for example, "8+2=10; 8+5=13; 8+3=11;" and so forth. Or, looking at row 8 and saying fact families in random order, you can say, "8+4=12; 4+8=12; 12-8=4; 12-4=8; 8+7=15; 7+8=15; 15-8-7; 15-7=8," and so forth.

4. You can look over the table for the facts that you are shakiest on, and say the addition facts or fact families just for those. For example, you look at the table and decide you're a little shaky on 7+4. You say, "7+4=11; 4+7=11; 11-7=4; 11-4=7." Then you look some more and decide you're shaky on 9+7. You say, "9+7=16, 7+9=16; 16-9=7; 16-7=9."

Chapter 12: Practicing Addition and Subtraction Facts with Numerals

Now that you've practiced addition and subtraction facts in ways that give you a visual image of the numbers involved, you're ready to do a lot more practicing, just using numerals, the squiggles that represent numbers.

For each of the following drills, practice just looking at the questions in order and saying the answer, as fast as you can.

I want to talk a little bit about "as fast as you can." There's a key skill to learn here, which is how to move quickly without feeling flustered and anxious. Try to relax as you say the answers quickly. If you can move along fast without getting tense and stressed, you will be practicing a skill that will help you in all sorts of things other than math facts!

Here's a way to see how many you can do per minute, especially if you are doing this with a tutor. You start going, and you go for one minute. If you get to the end of the set of problems, you start over again at the beginning without pausing.

Let's first practice with the plus 0's and plus 1's, addition and subtraction. This is a batch we didn't feel we needed to memorize. But don't feel bad if you start out slowly and need to pick up speed with more practice.

Learning the Math Facts

Adding and subtracting 0 and 1

1. 0+7=
2. 1+1=
3. 0-0=
4. 3+0=
5. 3-3=
6. 1+6=
7. 1+0=
8. 1-0=
9. 1+2=
10. 7-6=
11. 8-0=
12. 0+0=
13. 4-3=
14. 0+2=
15. 2-2=
16. 5-1=
17. 1+3=
18. 7-7=
19. 2-1=
20. 1+7=
21. 4+0=
22. 0+5=
23. 3-1=
24. 4-0=
25. 7-1=
26. 6+0=
27. 9-8=
28. 4+1=
29. 8-7=
30. 9+0=
31. 5-4=
32. 7+1=
33. 9-1=
34. 6-6=
35. 6-5=
36. 0+8=
37. 5+1=
38. 9-9=

The Plus 10's

Adding a one digit number to 10 should be pretty easy – all you have to do is put a 1 in front of the number. For example to add 2+10, just put a one in front of the 2; you get 12. To add 10+7, you put a 1 in front of the 7 and get 17.

The subtraction facts for the 10s fit into the fact families just as they have before. For example, since

10+5=15, then
5+10=15
15-5=10
15-10=5.

Chapter 12: Practicing Addition and Subtraction Facts with Numerals

Here's another fact family with 4 members:

10+7=17
7+10=17
17-7=10
17-10=7.

Now let's practice the facts in the plus 10 family. See how rapidly you can say them.

1. 10+2=
2. 11-1=
3. 13-3=
4. 17-10=
5. 15-10=
6. 3+10=
7. 13-8=
8. 11-10=
9. 13-10=
10. 15-5=
11. 4+10=
12. 10+5=
13. 6+10=
14. 12-2=
15. 16-10=
16. 12-10=
17. 19-9=
18. 10+7=
19. 8+10=
20. 16-6=
21. 18-10=
22. 14-4=
23. 19-10=
24. 17-7=
25. 10+9=
26. 14-10=

The Plus 2's

You've already practiced the plus twos a lot with the broken number lines and the dominoes. Here's another way to remember them. Can you count by 2's? It's like regular counting, only you skip a number each time. If you start with 0, you skip 1 and say 2; you skip 3 and say 4, and so forth. It goes 2, 4, 6, 8, 10, 12, 14, 16, 18, 20, and so forth. If you start with 1, it goes 1, 3, 5, 7, 9, 11, 13, 15, 17, 19, and so forth. It's good to be able to count with these sequences. Practice until you can count by

Learning the Math Facts

2's without having to think much about it -- where it's very automatic. You may even want to see how quickly you can count by 2's to 100.

2, 4, 6, 8, 10 and so forth are the even numbers. 1, 3, 5, 7, 9, 11, and so forth are the odd numbers.

So when we add two to any even number, the answer is just the next even number. When we add two to any odd number, the answer is the next odd number.

Or, if you don't want to think about counting by twos and even and odd numbers, you can just count two up from any number to add two. For example, for 9+2, we say 10 (which is one up) and then 11 (which is two up, and our answer). For 6+2 we can say to ourselves, 7, 8. 8 is our answer.

Now let's practice the 2s using numerals.

1. 2+2=
2. 6-4=
3. 9-2=
4. 2+5=
5. 3-1=
6. 6-2=
7. 4-2=
8. 2+4=
9. 3+2=
10. 5-3=
11. 6+2=
12. 7-5=
13. 8-2=
14. 2+6=
15. 8-6=
16. 4+2=
17. 5-2=
18. 9-7=
19. 2+7=
20. 7-2=
21. 10-8=
22. 8+2=
23. 2+9=
24. 5-2=
25. 3-2=
26. 5+2=

Chapter 12: Practicing Addition and Subtraction Facts with Numerals

The Doubles

Please notice the pattern of the answers for the math facts that are doubles:

1+1=2	2-1=1
2+2=4	4-2=2
3+3=6	6-3=3
4+4=8	8-4=4
5+5=10	10-5=5
6+6=12	12-6=6
7+7=14	14-7=7
8+8=16	16-8=8
9+9=18	18-9=9
10+10=20	20-10=10

The answers for addition, in the left columns, skip count by twos, don't they? And the answers for subtraction, in the right column, count by ones.

A good exercise to do is to say the addition doubles in order, several times, and then the subtraction doubles in order, several times. Now let's practice the doubles in random order.

1. 6+6=
2. 3+3=
3. 7+7=
4. 4+4=
5. 8+8=
6. 5+5=
7. 9+9=
8. 3+3=
9. 10-5=
10. 20-10=
11. 16-8=
12. 7+7=
13. 8-4=
14. 2-1=
15. 9+9=
16. 2+2=
17. 14-7=
18. 4-2=
19. 8+8=
20. 5+5=
21. 18-9=
22. 10+10=
23. 4+4=
24. 12-6=
25. 6-3=
26. 6+6=

The One Aparts

The "one aparts" are the math facts where the two numbers added are one apart from each other. They are:

2 and 3
3 and 4
4 and 5
5 and 6
6 and 7
7 and 8
8 and 9

One way some people remember the one aparts is that the sum is one more than the double for the lower number. So for example, when doing 3+4, we remember that 3+3=6. 3+4 has to be one more than that, since 4 is one more than 3. So since 3+3=6, 3+4=7.

Thus
Since   2+2=4,   2+3=5.
Since   3+3=6,   3+4=7.
Since   4+4=8,   4+5=9.
Since   5+5=10,   5+6=11.
Since   6+6=12,   6+7=13.
Since   7+7=14,   7+8=15.
Since   8+8=16,   8+9=17.

It's good to say these in order. Afterwards, practice the one aparts in random order, as below.

Chapter 12: Practicing Addition and Subtraction Facts with Numerals

One aparts

1. 5+4=
2. 6+7=
3. 3+4=
4. 8+7=
5. 5+6=
6. 4+3=
7. 4+5=
8. 6+5=
9. 7+8=
10. 7+6=
11. 8+9
12. 5+6=
13. 15-7=
14. 9-4=
15. 4+3=
16. 8+7=
17. 13-7=
18. 7-3=
19. 11-5=
20. 3+4=
21. 17-8=
22. 5+4=
23. 7+8=
24. 6+5=
25. 7-4=
26. 17-9=
27. 13-6=
28. 9-5=
29. 4+5=
30. 15-8=
31. 6+7=
32. 11-6=

The Plus 9's

Adding 9 to a number is the same as adding 10 to one less than that number. That's because 9 is one less than 10! Below are some to practice in random order.

1. 9+5=
2. 6+9=
3. 9+3=
4. 8+9=
5. 9+7=
6. 3+9=
7. 9+4=
8. 9+8=
9. 7+9=
10. 5+9=
11. 9+6=
12. 9+5=
13. 6+9=
14. 15-9=
15. 12-9=
16. 14-5=
17. 9+3=
18. 11-9=
19. 12-3=
20. 9+2=
21. 8+9=
22. 9+7=
23. 3+9=
24. 13-9=
25. 11-2=
26. 17-8=
27. 14-9=
28. 9+4=
29. 16-9=
30. 13-4=
31. 9+8=
32. 17-9=
33. 15-6=
34. 7+9=
35. 5+9=
36. 16-7=
37. 9+6=

Chapter 12: Practicing Addition and Subtraction Facts with Numerals

The Plus 8s

Adding 8 to any number is the same as adding 10 to 2 less than the number. That's because 10-2 is 8!

So for example, suppose we're adding 8+3. 2 less than 3 is 1, so the answer is 11. For 8+4, two less than 4 is 2, so the answer is 12. For 8+5, two less than 5 is 3, so the answer is 13. And so forth.

Let's practice with plus 8s, including the subtraction facts in the same family.

Plus 8s

1. 8+6=
2. 3+8=
3. 8+2=
4. 8+9=
5. 11-3=
6. 7+8=
7. 5+8=
8. 8+4=
9. 12-4=
10. 2+8=
11. 8+7=
12. 10-2=
13. 8+8=
14. 4+8=
15. 11-8=
16. 6+8=
17. 16-8=
18. 10-8=
19. 9+8=
20. 8+3=
21. 17-8=
22. 14-6=
23. 13-8=
24. 8+5=
25. 15-8=
26. 17-9=
27. 14-8=
28. 12-8=
29. 15-7=
30. 13-5=

The Two Aparts

"Two aparts" are numbers like 5+3, 4+6, 7+9, and so forth. If you want to, you can remember these by figuring that they are the same as the double of the number in between them. For example, if we have 5+3, we could take one away from the 5 (making it 4) and give that one to the 3 (making it 4). So 5+3 is the same as 4+4. By the same reasoning, 6+4 is the same as 5+5. 7+5 is the same as 6+6. 8+6 is the same as 7+7. And so forth.

1. 5+3=
2. 5+7=
3. 8+6=
4. 3+5=
5. 6+4=
6. 6-2=
7. 4+6=
8. 7+5=
9. 6+8=
10. 5+3=
11. 5+7=
12. 10-4=
13. 7+9=
14. 8-5=
15. 2+4=
16. 8+6=
17. 3+5=
18. 14-6=
19. 12-7=
20. 4+2=
21. 8-3=
22. 6+4=
23. 9+7=
24. 6-4=
25. 12-5=
26. 4+6=
27. 10-6=
28. 14-8=
29. 16-9=
30. 7+5=
31. 6+8=
32. 16-7=

Chapter 12: Practicing Addition and Subtraction Facts with Numerals

The Make 10s and Their Siblings

There are only three facts we haven't practiced yet in this chapter. Here they are:

3+6=9
3+7=10
4+7=11

One of these, 7+3, is a "make 10": a pair of numbers that add up to 10. The make 10s are 1+9, 2+8, 3+7, 4+6, and 5+5, and their family members. Knowing these facts really well helps some people in remembering facts like 7+4. (They may think: since 6+4=10, and 7 is one more than 6, 7+4 has to be one more than 10!) You want to just remember 7+4 like a flash and not have to go through all this. But I want to give you several different tools to remember the facts, and knowing the facts that make 10 is useful in any case.)

6+3=9 is also a "sibling" of 6+4=10. You can remember that 3+6=9 by remembering that 4+6=10, and that since 3 is one less than 4, 3+6 has to be one less than 10, or 9.

This next drill is on the sums to 10 as well as 6+3 and 7+4.

1. 6+3=
2. 4+7=
3. 3+6=
4. 7+3=
5. 7+4=
6. 3+7=
7. 1-4=
8. 10-7=
9. 4+7=
10. 9-6=
11. 3+6=
12. 11-7=
13. 9-3=
14. 10-3=
15. 7+3=
16. 7+4=
17. 3+7=
18. 1+9=
19. 6+4=
20. 7+3=
21. 8+2=
22. 5+5=
23. 3+7=
24. 10-2=
25. 10-6=
26. 10-5=
27. 10-3=
28. 10-8=
29. 10-7=
30. 10-4=
31. 2+8=

More drill on addition and subtraction with the basic 36 families

Here's an all-purpose number line to use for the following problems if you need it; by now I hope you won't need to.

0 1 2 3 4 5 6 7 8 9 10 11 12 13 14 15 16 17 18 19 20

Here are the 36 addition facts we set out to memorize, in random order:

1. 6+7=
2. 2+6=
3. 4+8=
4. 4+5=
5. 5+9=
6. 2+3=
7. 3+9=
8. 3+7=
9. 6+9=
10. 4+9=
11. 4+7=
12. 6+8=
13. 2+5=
14. 7+9=
15. 6+6=
16. 3+5=
17. 5+8=
18. 7+7=
19. 2+3=
20. 8+8=
21. 5+6=
22. 7+8=
23. 3+8=
24. 9+9=
25. 2+4=
26. 4+6=
27. 5+7=
28. 3+6=
29. 4+4=
30. 8+9=
31. 3+3=
32. 2+9=
33. 2+8=
34. 5+5=
35. 3+4=
36. 2+7=

Chapter 12: Practicing Addition and Subtraction Facts with Numerals

Here's the number line again:

0 1 2 3 4 5 6 7 8 9 10 11 12 13 14 15 16 17 18 19 20

And here are 36 subtraction facts, one from each family of the 36 addition facts given above.

1. 13-6=
2. 8-2=
3. 12-4=
4. 9-4=
5. 14-5=
6. 5-2=
7. 12-3=
8. 10-3=
9. 15-6=
10. 13-4=
11. 11-4=
12. 14-6=
13. 7-2=
14. 16-7=
15. 12-6=
16. 8-3=
17. 13-5=
18. 14-7=
19. 5-2=
20. 16-8=
21. 11-5=
22. 15-7=
23. 11-3=
24. 18-9=
25. 6-2=
26. 10-4=
27. 12-5=
28. 9-3=
29. 8-4=
30. 17-8=
31. 6-3=
32. 11-2=
33. 10-2=
34. 10-5=
35. 7-3=
36. 9-2=

Learning the Math Facts

Here's the number line again:

0 1 2 3 4 5 6 7 8 9 10 11 12 13 14 15 16 17 18 19 20

And here are 36 more subtraction facts, the other from each family of the 36 addition facts given before.

1. 13-7=
2. 8-6=
3. 12-8=
4. 9-5=
5. 14-9=
6. 5-3=
7. 12-9=
8. 10-7=
9. 15-9=
10. 13-9=
11. 11-7=
12. 14-8=
13. 7-5=
14. 16-9=
15. 12-6=
16. 8-5=
17. 13-8=
18. 14-7=
19. 5-3=
20. 16-8=
21. 11-6=
22. 15-8=
23. 11-8=
24. 18-9=
25. 6-4=
26. 10-6=
27. 12-7=
28. 9-6=
29. 8-4=
30. 17-9=
31. 6-3=
32. 11-9=
33. 10-8=
34. 10-5=
35. 7-4=
36. 9-7=

Chapter 13: Addition Work That's Useful for Multiplication

What is multiplication? It can be thought of as repeated addition. So 2+2+2 is the same as 2 three times, or 3 times 2. 5+5+5+5 is adding up four 5's, or four times five. In this section we're going to practice addition and subtraction in ways that make us land on the numbers that are the answers to the multiplication facts.

Review of regrouping or "carrying" when adding

How do you do an addition problem like 28+7? We can think of 28 as 2 tens and 8 ones. 8 ones plus 7 more ones gives 15 ones. But we can think of 15 as increasing the number of tens we have from 2 to 3, and leaving 5 ones left over. So the answer is 35.

Here's another example:

```
  49
 +7
```

To do this, we add 9+7, and get 16. We write down the 6, and "carry" the 1 over to the tens column. 4+1 is 5; we write down the 5 and come to our final answer of 56.

```
  1
 49
 +7
 56
```

Regrouping when subtracting, or "borrowing"

Suppose we want to subtract 72-8.

```
  6 12
  7̶2̶
  -8
  ──
  64
```

When we start to subtract, we don't have enough ones to subtract 8 from 2. So we unbundle or "borrow" one of the 10s in 72, to make 72 into 6 tens and 12 ones. Now we subtract 8 from 12 and get 4; we don't subtract anything from the 6, but just bring it down. So 64 is our answer.

The skip-counting sequences

Now let's practice some repeated addition. When we do these, we'll always start with 0. Let's add 2 each time.

1. 0+2=2
2. 2+2=4
3. 4+2=6
4. 6+2=8
5. 8+2=10
6. 10+2=12
7. 12+2=14
8. 14+2=16
9. 16+2=18
10. 18+2=20

Chapter 13: Addition Work That's Useful for Multiplication

Notice that in line 2, we have added up 2 2's, and the answer is 4. That means that 2 x 2=4. By the time we reach line 5, we have added up 5 2's; the answer is 10. That means that 5 x 2 = 10.

Let's do the same thing with 3's.

1. 0+3=3
2. 3+3=6
3. 6+3=9
4. 9+3=12
5. 12+3=15
6. 15+3=18
7. 18+3=21
8. 21+3=24
9. 24+3=27
10. 27+3=30

Can you see how the answers we got when we did this are the answers to multiplication questions? Suppose we get 3 of something. Then we get 3 more – now we have 3 x 2, or 6. We get 3 more; now we have 3 x 3, or 9. And so on. Let's write the multiplication facts for 3's, using the answers to the addition problems above.

3 x 1 = 3
3 x 2 = 6
3 x 3 = 9
3 x 4 = 12
3 x 5 = 15
3 x 6 = 18
3 x 7 = 21
3 x 8 = 24
3 x 9 = 27
3 x 10 = 30

Do you see that the answers are always three more than the previous answer?

Let's do the same thing with 4's.

1. 0+4=4
2. 4+4=8
3. 8+4=12
4. 12+4=16
5. 16+4=20
6. 20+4=24
7. 24+4=28
8. 28+4=32
9. 32+4=36
10. 36+4=40

The answers we get to these addition problems correspond to the 4 times table:

4 x 1 = 4
4 x 2 = 8
4 x 3 = 12
4 x 4 = 16
4 x 5 = 20
4 x 6 = 24
4 x 7 = 28
4 x 8 = 32
4 x 9 = 36
4 x 10 = 40

With the 5's, let's save ourselves some writing by just starting with 0 and adding 5, several times, to our previous answer:

0, 5, 10, 15, 20, 25, 30, 35, 40, 45, 50.

Adding 5 each time is called skip-counting by 5's. What we did previously was skip-counting by 2's, 3's, and 4's.

Now let's add 6 each time, again starting with 0, and finishing when we get to 60.

0, 6, 12, 18, 24, 30, 36, 42, 48, 54, 60.

We had to do a fair amount of regrouping to do that, didn't we? There's more regrouping to come.

Let's do the 7's.

0, 7, 14, 21, 28, 35, 42, 49, 56, 63, 70.

And the 8's.

0, 8, 16, 24, 32, 40, 48, 56, 64, 72, 80.

And the 9's.

0, 9, 18, 27, 36, 45, 54, 63, 72, 81, 90.

And finally the 10's.

0, 10, 20, 30, 40, 50, 60, 70, 80, 90, 100.

    If you can do the addition problems fast enough to figure out the skip-counts, you can figure out the answer to any multiplication fact. For example, if you want to know 8 x 4, you can say "8" and put up one finger; say "16" and put up another to make 2 fingers; say "24" as you put up one more to have 3 fingers up; and say "32" as you put your fourth finger up. Since you have counted up 4 8's, 32 is 4 x 8.

Let's practice with some of the addition problems that are necessary to do the skip counts. You can close your book and practice skip counting upward by adding the same number each time. Practice doing it for the 2's through the 10's.

Below are some of the addition problems you use to skip count, only out of order. Practice getting fast with these; it will help you to get fast with the one-digit addition facts also.

1. 14+2=
2. 21+3=
3. 16+4=
4. 18+9=
5. 21+7=
6. 12+3=
7. 48+8=
8. 16+8=
9. 20+5=
10. 18+6=
11. 14+7=
12. 32+4=
13. 54+6=
14. 63+9=
15. 27+9=
16. 40+8=
17. 15+5=
18. 24+4=
19. 16+2=
20. 12+4=
21. 28+7=
22. 36+6=
23. 30+10=
24. 56+7=
25. 36+9=
26. 12+2=
27. 15+3=
28. 48+6=
29. 63+7=
30. 35+5=
31. 12+6=
32. 18+2=
33. 30+5=
34. 45+9=
35. 35+7=
36. 50+10=
37. 24+3=
38. 13+3=
39. 30+6=
40. 56+8=
41. 54+9=
42. 20+4=
43. 72+9=
44. 70+10=
45. 24+8=
46. 6+2=
47. 24+6=
48. 28+4=
49. 64+8=
50. 45+5=
51. 27+3=
52. 81+9=
53. 90+10=
54. 42+7=
55. 32+8=
56. 42+6=
57. 36+4=
58. 72+8=
59. 49+7=

Chapter 13: Addition Work That's Useful for Multiplication

After you've practiced with these, please go back and practice generating the skip counts. See if you are faster at the skip counts than before.

After you've done this some, please take a listen to some skip-counting songs I recorded and put on the internet. You can find them at optskills.org/songs.

Learning the Math Facts

Chapter 14: Four Rules That Cut Down on Memorization in Multiplication

In addition, we used four rules to cut down on memorization: one was that order didn't make a difference, and the other three had to do with adding 0, adding 1, and adding 10. In multiplication, we'll use four rules also: an order doesn't make a difference rule, and rules about multiplying by 0, 1, and 10.

Order doesn't make a difference in multiplication

Multiplication is "commutative," just as addition is. Commutative means that "order doesn't make a difference." So 3 x 4 is the same as 4 x 3. 2 x 4 is the same as 4 x 2.

Let's prove that to ourselves with an example of something repeated in rows and columns.

We have 4 asterisks in each row. And we have 2 rows. So we could skip count by 4's, saying "4, 8" to count how many we have. We've illustrated that 4 x 2 = 8.

Chapter 14: Four Rules That Cut Down on Memorization in Multiplication

But we also have 2 asterisks in each column. And we have 4 columns. So to skip-count how many we have, we could say "2, 4, 6, 8." We still arrive at 8 no matter which way we go: by adding 2, 4 times, or by adding 4, 2 times.

Any time we have something arranged in rows and columns, it shows us that order doesn't make a difference in multiplication. Let's look at another one.

We have 15 asterisks altogether. We have 5 in each row, and we have 3 rows. So this shows us that adding 3 5s gives 15, or 3 x 5 = 15. But we also have 3 in each column, and we have 5 columns. So adding up 3, 5 times, or 5 x 3, also equals 15. 5 groups of 3 and 3 groups of 5 are the same.

We know that since there's only one set of asterisks that we're talking about, any way of counting them should land on the same total number. Just looking at the picture proves to us that taking 5 three times is the same as taking 3 five times.

The fact that order doesn't make a difference cuts way down on the number of multiplication facts we have to learn. Once we've learned 5 x 3, we don't have to learn 3 x 5 all over again.

Multiplying by zero

What is 0+0+0+0+0+0? Still 0, isn't it? No matter how many 0s we add together, we still get 0.

Remember that multiplication is just repeated addition. So this means that 6 x 0 is 0, 7 x 0 is 0, 2 x 0 is 0, and any number multiplied by zero is 0.

The rule that anything times zero is zero means we don't have to memorize 8 x 0 or 0 x 8 or zero times anything else.

Multiplying by one

Let's represent 3 x 1 by having 3 asterisks in each row, for a total of 1 row.

*   *   *

How many do we have in all? Three! When we multiply any number by 1, we get the same number we started with. Any number times 1 is the number itself.

So we don't have to memorize 8 x 1 or 1 x 8. We know the answer is 8 in each case.

Chapter 14: Four Rules That Cut Down on Memorization in Multiplication

Multiplying by 10

10 x 2 is 20. 10 x 3 is 30. 10 x 4 is 40. Do you know the rule for multiplying any whole number by 10? You just add a 0 to the number. 10*5=50. 10*6=60. 8*10=80, and 9*10=90.

Now we've reduced the number of multiplication facts we need to memorize from 121 to 36! Here are those 36:

1. 2*2=4	12. 6*3=18	25. 8*5=40
	13. 6*4=24	26. 8*6=48
2. 3*2=6	14. 6*5=30	27. 8*7=56
3. 3*3=9	15. 6*6=36	28. 8*8=64
4. 4*2=8	16. 7*2=14	29. 9*2=18
5. 4*3=12	17. 7*3=21	30. 9*3=27
6. 4*4=16	18. 7*4=28	31. 9*4=36
	19. 7*5=35	32. 9*5=45
7. 5*2=10	20. 7*6=42	33. 9*6=54
8. 5*3=15	21. 7*7=49	34. 9*7=63
9. 5*4=20		35. 9*8=72
10. 5*5=25	22. 8*2=16	36. 9*9=81
	23. 8*3=24	
11. 6*2=12	24. 8*4=32	

Practicing with some of the multiplication facts we've left out

Let's practice with some of the multiplication facts we don't have to memorize if we understand the rules given earlier in this chapter.

1. 6*0=
2. 7*1=
3. 8*10=
4. 4*0=

5. 2*1=
6. 9*10=
7. 7*10=
8. 5*1=

9. 8*0=
10. 3*10=
11. 3*0=
12. 3*1=

Chapter 15: Multiplying Using an Ordinary Number Line

If we want to visualize multiplication, we can use an ordinary number line. Suppose we start owning 0 apples. Someone gives us 4 bags, with 3 apples in each bag. The first bag gets us from owning 0 to owning 3, which we represent by the first jump on the number line, from 0 to 3. The second bag gets us from 3 to 6 (we count 1, 2, 3 as we jump to 4, 5, and 6). The third bag gets us from 6 to 9, and the 4th bag from 9 to 12. So all 4 bags with 3 in each bag yield 12 apples in all.

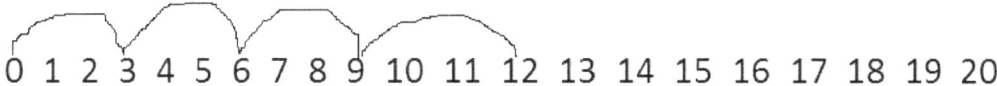

Try visualizing multiplication yourself, using an ordinary number line. How about 2 * 3? You can do 3 jumps of 2 each. The first jump gets you to 2, the second to 4, and the third to 6. So 2 * 3 =6. Or, if you want, you can have two jumps of three each. The first lands you on 3, and the second lands you on 6.

0 1 2 3 4 5 6 7 8 9 10 11 12 13 14 15 16 17 18 19 20

Do a few more. How about 3 * 3?
4 * 4?
6 * 3?
4 * 5?

If you were to do 9 * 8 or 9 * 9, you'd need a lot longer number line, wouldn't you? And it also would get tedious counting out so many jumps, so many times. This is why we'll go to broken number lines.

Chapter 16: Multiplying Using Broken Number Lines

We made pictures of multiplication earlier, using rows and columns of things like the picture below. (We're going to use ampersands this time instead of asterisks.)

    &   &   &
    &   &   &

This picture shows 2 rows, with 3 things in each row. It illustrates the fact that 2 * 3 = 6. Notice that there are 6 things in this picture; they are in two groups of 3, or three groups of 2.

What about this picture:

& & & & & & & & &
& & & & & & & & &
& & & & & & & & &
& & & & & & & & &
& & & & & & & & &
& & & & & & & & &

How many rows and how many columns are there? You can count them, but it's kind of tedious, and it's easy to make a mistake. It's not obvious from this picture what is being multiplied by what, and how many there are altogether. This picture illustrates that 6*9=54, because there are 6 rows with 9 in each row, and 54 things altogether. (There are also 9 columns with 6 in each column.)

Chapter 16: Multiplying Using Broken Number Lines

Instead of picturing a bunch of asterisks or ampersands that are tedious to count, how about if we picture the same arrangement of numerals? We can let the numerals do the counting for us.
Here we go with picturing 2 * 3 = 6.

   1 2 3
   4 5 6

We still have 6 things in this picture, but now they're 6 numerals. There are 3 in the first row, and three in the second row, for a total of 6 of them. This demonstrates that 2 * 3 = 6, using two sets of three things for a total of 6 of them.

How about the second picture we used above? Let's replace the rows and columns of ampersands with rows and columns of numbers. And let's number the rows, so we don't have to count them.

Row 1.	1	2	3	4	5	6	7	8	9
Row 2.	10	11	12	13	14	15	16	17	18
Row 3.	19	20	21	22	23	24	25	26	27
Row 4.	28	29	30	31	32	33	34	35	36
Row 5.	37	38	39	40	41	42	43	44	45
Row 6.	46	47	48	49	50	51	52	53	54

Now is it clearer what multiplication fact we're making a picture of? There are 9 things (numbers) in each row, and there are 6 rows. We have 9, six times. And we have a total of 54 of them. (54 is the last thing in the last row.) So we're showing that 6 x 9 = 54.

Now we're going to do something important. We're going to let arrays illustrate several different multiplication facts, by looking at a certain number of rows, starting from the top, and ignoring the rest. Suppose, in the picture above that goes from 1 to 54, you ignore the last row, and just look at the first 5 rows. In those rows there are 9 things, 5 times. At the end of these 5 rows is the number 45. So these 5 rows show that 9 x 5 is 45. By looking at the first 5 rows and ignoring row six, we can visualize the multiplication fact, 9 x 5= 45.

The first 4 rows have 36 numbers in them, and they show that 9 x 4=36. The first three show that 9 x 3=27, the first two that 9 x2 =18, and the first 1 row shows that 9 x 1=9. We see from this that we don't need a new picture for each multiplication fact. The first row illustrates 9 x 1. The first two rows illustrate 9 x 2. The first 3 rows illustrate 9 x 3. By ignoring all the rows after a certain number, we can avoid a lot of copying over of these arrays.

When we use the broken number line arrays to see the multiplication facts, we really only use the last column, that is the one on the far right, to get the answers to the multiplication facts. If you look down that column, you will see the numbers you land on are the skip-counts. Those are all you really need to retrieve the multiplication facts. But I think that it's good to see the whole array, so that over and over, you can see how the answers to multiplication fact problems are connected to that most basic mathematical operation: counting by ones! When you use these broken number lines, seeing all the numbers, not just the skip-counting answers, will give you a mental image of how big each of the numbers you are talking about is. When you see a representation, say, of 4 rows with 9 in each row, you are really looking at 4, 9, and 36. There are 4 rows. There are 9 columns. There are 36 numbers.

Chapter 16: Multiplying Using Broken Number Lines

Now let's go through and picture the multiplication facts you need to memorize. This time through, we're going to stop each array when we get to a number multiplied by itself. Rather than a "double," these are called "perfect squares."

The 2s:

Row 1:   1   2
Row 2:   3   4

The array above shows us that 2 rows of two things in each row gives us 4 things altogether, or 2 x 2 = 4.

The 3s:

Row 1:   1   2   3
Row 2:   4   5   6
Row 3:   7   8   9

The first two rows of the array above show us that 3 x 2 = 6. The first three rows show us that 3 x 3 = 9.

Let's use the same steps that we used with the addition facts, while you look at the array of 3's above. First just say the facts in order: 3x1=3, 3x2=6, 3x3=9, and then start over.

Second, say the facts in random order: for example, 3x2=6, 3x1=3, 3x3=9, 3x1=3, and so forth. Do this looking at the picture.

Third, say the facts in order, looking away from the picture, looking back at it if you need to.

Fourth, say the facts in random order, looking away from the picture, looking back at it if you need to.

The 4s:

Row 1:	1	2	3	4
Row 2:	5	6	7	8
Row 3:	9	10	11	12
Row 4:	13	14	15	16

The first two rows show that 4 x 2 =8. The first 3 rows show that 4 x 3= 12. The first 4 rows show us that 4 * 4 = 16.
Please go through the same four steps as before.

1. Say the facts in order, looking at the picture. 4 x 1=4. 4 x 2= 8. 4 x 3=12. 4 x 4=16.
2. Say the facts in random order, looking at the picture.
3. Say the facts in order, only looking if you need to.
4. Say the facts in random order, only looking if you need to.

The 5s:

Row 1:	1	2	3	4	5
Row 2:	6	7	8	9	10
Row 3:	11	12	13	14	15
Row 4:	16	17	18	19	20
Row 5:	21	22	23	24	25

Again, please go through the 4 steps: facts in order, looking; facts in random order, looking; facts in order, looking only when necessary; facts in random order, looking only when necessary.

Chapter 16: Multiplying Using Broken Number Lines

The 6s:

Row 1:	1	2	3	4	5	6
Row 2:	7	8	9	10	11	12
Row 3:	13	14	15	16	17	18
Row 4:	19	20	21	22	23	24
Row 5:	25	26	27	28	29	30
Row 6:	31	32	33	34	35	36

Again, 4 steps: 1. in order, looking. 2. at random, looking. 3. in order, looking away. 4. at random, looking away.

The 7s:

Row 1:	1	2	3	4	5	6	7
Row 2:	8	9	10	11	12	13	14
Row 3:	15	16	17	18	19	20	21
Row 4:	22	23	24	25	26	27	28
Row 5:	29	30	31	32	33	34	35
Row 6:	36	37	38	39	40	41	42
Row 7:	43	44	45	46	47	48	49

Again, please do the 4 steps with the 7s.

The 8s:

Row 1:	1	2	3	4	5	6	7	8
Row 2:	9	10	11	12	13	14	15	16
Row 3:	17	18	19	20	21	22	23	24
Row 4:	25	26	27	28	29	30	31	32
Row 5:	33	34	35	36	37	38	39	40
Row 6:	41	42	43	44	45	46	47	48
Row 7:	49	50	51	52	53	54	55	56
Row 8:	57	58	59	60	61	62	63	64

Again, do the 4 steps with the 8s. Notice that the ones digit goes down by 2 each time. This is because 8 is 10-2. So to add 8, you can add 10 and subtract 2.

Chapter 16: Multiplying Using Broken Number Lines

For the 9's, notice that as you go in order, the 10's digit goes up by 1 each time, and the 1's digit goes down by 1. This is because adding 9 is the same as adding 10 and subtracting 1. Also please notice that all the answers have digits that add up to 9, and that if you want to multiply 9 by any one digit number, the first digit of the answer is one less than the number you're multiplying by. For example, for 9 x 3, the first digit of the answer (27) is 2. For 9 x 4, the first digit of the answer (36) is 3. And so forth. The second digit is 9 minus the first digit, since the two digits have to had to 9.

The 9s:

Row 1:	1	2	3	4	5	6	7	8	9
Row 2:	10	11	12	13	14	15	16	17	18
Row 3:	19	20	21	22	23	24	25	26	27
Row 4:	28	29	30	31	32	33	34	35	36
Row 5:	37	38	39	40	41	42	43	44	45
Row 6:	46	47	48	49	50	51	52	53	54
Row 7:	55	56	57	58	59	60	61	62	63
Row 8:	64	65	66	67	68	69	70	71	72
Row 9:	73	74	75	76	77	78	79	80	81

Finally, do the 4 steps with the 9s. Again, the 4 steps are: facts in order looking; facts in random order looking; facts in order not looking; facts in random order not looking.

When you're done with this, and you can do all the steps very quickly, with all the different arrays, congratulations! You've learned the multiplication facts!

We're going to do more work on them, though, work that will hopefully get these facts even more strongly into your memory. First, we're going to think about division, the relation of division to multiplication, and multiplication and division fact families.

Chapter 17: Division, and Its Relation to Multiplication

Let's look at another set of asterisks in rows and columns. (Remember, the rows go horizontally, or from left to right, and the columns go vertically, or up and down.)

This array illustrates that two groups of three make 6 (if we count the rows as groups). In other words, 2 x 3 =6. It also illustrates that three groups of two make 6 (if we count the columns as groups). In other words, 3 x 2 = 6.

But the asterisks above also illustrate the answer to a different sort of question. Suppose the question is: "If we take 6 things, and divide them into two equal groups, how many are in each group?" The two rows above already are two equal groups. There are 3 in each of those groups. So the answer to the question is, "3." Two ways to write this are:

6 ÷ 2 = 3   or 6 / 2 = 3.

The asterisks also illustrate the answer to another question: "If we take 6 things, and divide them into 3 equal groups, how many are in each group?" The three columns above are already show us 3 equal groups. There are 2 in each of those groups. So the answer to "If you divide 6 into 3 equal groups, how many do you get?" is 2. We write this as:

6 ÷ 3 = 2 or 6 / 3 = 2.

There's another way to ask questions that are answered by division. The question is: "If we start with 6 things, and divide them into groups of 2, how many groups will we come out with?" Imagine yourself drawing one circle around the two in the first column, a second around the 2 in the second column, and a third circle around the 2 in the 3rd column. We come out with 3 circles, or 3 groups, and that's our answer. The asterisks illustrate 6 ÷ 2 = 3 or 6 / 2 = 3.

We could ask, "If we start with 6 things, and divide them into groups of 3, how many groups will we come out with?" We could draw a circle around the three in the first row, and a second circle around the 3 in the second row. We get 2 groups. So 6 ÷ 3 = 2 or 6 / 3 = 2.

So with multiplication, we are given the number of groups and the number in each group. We want to know the total number.

With division, we are given the total number. We are also given either the number of groups, or the number in each group. Whichever one of those two is missing, we find by division.

Here's a table showing what we've just said:

Chapter 17: Division, and Its Relation to Multiplication

Multiplication:

Given #1	Given #2	Missing – we find
number of groups	number in each group	Total number

Division:

Given #1	Given #2	Missing – we find
Total number	number of groups	number in each group
Total number	number in each group	number of groups

Here's one concrete example of all this.

Multiplication (finding total): We have 3 bags. There are 4 apples in each bag. How many apples total? Answer: 3 x 4 = 12.

Division (finding number in each group): We have 12 apples. We divide them equally into 3 groups. How many in each group? Answer: 12/3 = 4 in each group.

Division (finding number of groups): We have 12 apples. We divide them into groups of 4. How many groups do we get? Answer: 12/4 = 3 groups.

This isn't easy stuff. It's a lot harder to really understand this than to memorize facts. But it's worthwhile thinking about this until you really fully understand it.

    Before we stop thinking about how division and multiplication are related, let's think about the fact that division can "undo" multiplication. Let's start with a certain number, like 3. Let's multiply it by any number. How about 5? That gets us to 15. Now let's divide 15 by 5. That gets us back to 3. So if we multiply by a number, and divide what we get by the same number, we get back where we started! The word we use to say that division "undoes" multiplication is the word "inverse": division is the inverse of multiplication.

    Let's go somewhere and back again by multiplication and division one more time, just to illustrate again how division is the opposite, or the inverse, of multiplication. Let's start with 2. Let's first multiply it by 3, and then divide what we get by 3. Any guesses as to where we'll wind up? Let's see. 2 x 3 is 6. 6 divided by 3 is 2. We started with 2, and when we multiplied and and divided by the same number, we ended up where we started!

Chapter 17: Division, and Its Relation to Multiplication

Chapter 18: Reducing Memorization Of Division Facts

Fact Families

As we discussed in the previous chapter, once you know a multiplication fact, you can figure out one more multiplication fact and two division facts from it (if the two numbers being multiplied are different). For example, if you know that

7x5=35,

then it follows that

5x7=35,

and that
35/5=7
and
35/7=5.

For another example: if we know that 5x 4=20, then we also know that 4x5=20 and that 20/4=5 and 20/5=4.

Dividing 0 by any number, and not dividing by 0

0 divided by any number (other than 0) gives 0. For example, we have 3 people among which to divide money. But we have no money. How much does each person get? Nothing! This tells us that 0 divided

into 3 equal parts gives 0, or that 0/3 =0. Similarly, 0/5=0, 0/8=0, and so forth.

What about a problem like 5/0? To ask what is 5 divided by 0 is like saying, "How many times do you have to add 0 together, before you get 5?" But no matter how many times we add 0s, we'll never get anything other than 0 – we'll never get to 5. So the question, "What is 5 divided by 0" has no answer. We say that "Division by zero is not allowed."

Dividing by 1, and dividing a number by itself

Dividing any number by 1 gives the number itself. For example, 8/1=8.   27 divided by 1 gives 27.

Dividing any number by itself gives 1. For example, 8/8=1. 6/6=1. And so forth.

Dividing numbers ending in 0 by 10

To divide a number ending in 0 by 10, you just knock off the 0 that the number ends with. For example, 60/10=6. 80/10=8. 50/10=5. And so forth.

Dividing numbers ending in 0 from 10 to 90 by the number in the tens' place

It's easier to understand examples of this. Since 60/10=6, 60/6=10. Similarly, 90/9=10, 80/8=10, 20/2=10, and so forth.

Practice with division facts these rules teach us

Chapter 18: Reducing Memorization Of Division Facts

Let's practice with some division facts we don't need to memorize if we understand the rules given above.

1. 7/1=
2. 5/5=
3. 4/1=
4. 6/6=
5. 60/10=

6. 60/6=
7. 7/7=
8. 9/1=
9. 90/10=
10. 70/10=

11. 90/9=
12. 70/7=

Chapter 19: Multiplication and Division Fact Families

Addition and subtraction facts come in families of four, except for doubles, which are families of two. For multiplication and division, the fact families have four members except when a number is multiplied by itself – we call that a square. Let's think about the fact families that this array illustrates.

* * * *

* * * *

* * * *

There are 3 rows, and 4 in each row. We could also say there are 4 columns, with 3 in each column. There is a total of 12. So this array shows us that

3 x 4 = 12

and

4 x 3 = 12.

If we imagine that we looked at all 12, and divided them with 4 in each group, we would get 3 groups. Thus the same picture shows that

12 / 4 = 3.

And, if we imagine that we started with all 12, and divided them with 3 in each group, we would get 4 groups. Thus the same picture shows that

Chapter 19: Multiplication and Division Fact Families

12 / 3 = 4.

So there four members in this fact family, two multiplication and two division! What's the family, say, for 4 x 5 = 20? Here are all 4 family members:

4x5 = 20
5x4 = 20
20/4 = 5
20/5 = 4.

Now let's look at one of our arrays of numbers, let's say the 5s. This time we're going to continue the array all the way down to 10 rows.

The 5s:

Row 1:	1	2	3	4	5
Row 2:	6	7	8	9	10
Row 3:	11	12	13	14	15
Row 4:	16	17	18	19	20
Row 5:	21	22	23	24	25
Row 6:	26	27	28	29	30
Row 7:	31	32	33	34	35
Row 8:	36	37	38	39	40
Row 9:	41	42	43	44	45
Row 10:	46	47	48	49	50

What facts are illustrated by the numbers up to the end of the third row? The broken number line up to that point shows that:

1. 5 x 3 = 15 (because we have 3 groups with 5 in each group)
2. 3 x 5 = 15 (because we also have 5 groups with 3 in each group)
3. 15 / 3 = 5 (because when we make 3 groups, we have 5 in each)

Learning the Math Facts

4. 15 / 5 = 3. (because 5 in each group results in having 3 groups.)

What facts do the numbers up to the end of the 9th row illustrate? They show that

1. 5 x 9 = 45
2. 9 x 5 = 45
3. 45 / 5 = 9
4. 45 / 9 = 5

Do you get how to figure out all the fact families for any number of rows?

Here's our array again:

The 5s:

Row 1:	1	2	3	4	5
Row 2:	6	7	8	9	10
Row 3:	11	12	13	14	15
Row 4:	16	17	18	19	20
Row 5:	21	22	23	24	25
Row 6:	26	27	28	29	30
Row 7:	31	32	33	34	35
Row 8:	36	37	38	39	40
Row 9:	41	42	43	44	45
Row 10:	46	47	48	49	50

What facts are illustrated by the numbers up to the end of the fifth row? We see from them that:

1. 5 x 5 = 25
and

2. $25 / 5 = 5$.

Only two fact families are illustrated, with the number of rows and the number of columns are the same. This is very much like addition, where for example the fact family for $5 + 5 = 10$ is just

1. $5 + 5 = 10$
and
2. $10 - 5 = 5$.

Chapter 20: Multiplication Fact Families Using Broken Number Line Arrays

Here's our plan for this chapter. We're going to make an array going up to 10 for each of our numbers 2 through 9. Look at the array, look at the first row, and say the fact families for it. Look at the second row and do the same. Keep going through all 10 rows. I'll give you an example.

Here's the array for the times 2's.

Row 1:	1	2
Row 2:	3	4
Row 3:	5	6
Row 4:	7	8
Row 5:	9	10
Row 6:	11	12
Row 7:	13	14
Row 8:	15	16
Row 9:	17	18
Row 10:	19	20

So looking only at the first row, we say: "2 x 1 = 2. 1 x 2 = 2. 2/2=1. 2/1=2."
Looking at the second row, (and thinking about the numbers up to the end of the second row) we say "2*2=4. 4/2=2."
Looking at the third row, we say, "2*3=6. 3*2=6. 6/3=2. 6/2=3."
Looking at the fourth row, we say, "2*4=8. 4*2=8. 8/4=2. 8/2=4."
Looking at the fifth row, we say, "2*5=10. 5*2=10. 10/5=2. 10/2=5."

Chapter 20: Multiplication Fact Families Using Broken Number Line Arrays

And so forth! That's how you say the fact families in order, looking at the array.

The second step is to look at rows in random order and say the fact families. For example, we first look at row 8 and say "2*8=16. 8*2=16. 16/8=2. 16/2=8." Then we look at row 5 and say, "2*5=10. 5*2=10. 10/5=2. 10/2=5." We skip around and say fact families for random rows.

And that's it for this array, the one for the 2s! We're going to do the same thing for other arrays.

Learning the Math Facts

Let's work on the times 3's, using a similar array.

Row 1:   1   2   3
Row 2:   4   5   6
Row 3:   7   8   9
Row 4:   10   11   12
Row 5:   13   14   15
Row 6:   16   17   18
Row 7:   19   20   21
Row 8:   22   23   24
Row 9:   25   26   27
Row 10:   28   29   30

The plan is the same: start at the top, and say the fact family that each row (with the rows above it) illustrates.

So for row 1, say: "3*1=3. 1*3=3. 3/1=3. 3/3=1."
For row 2, say: "3*2=6. 2*3=6. 6/2=3. 6/3=2."
For row 3, say: "3*3=9. 9/3=3." (only two for this one.)

And so forth. Say them in order.
Then pick rows in random order, and say the fact families for each.

    Here's a reminder of what I want you to do with your brain while you're doing this. For example, when you do the 2*3=6 family, I want you to look at the first two rows and ignore the rest. I want you to see that there are really two groups of 3 objects – the first 2 rows, with 3 numbers in each. Then notice that there are 3 groups of 2 objects – the three columns, with 2 in each column. When you say the division facts,

Chapter 20: Multiplication Fact Families Using Broken Number Line Arrays

please notice that there are 6 things total, divided into 2 groups (the two rows) and there are 3 in each group. Also notice that there are 6 things, divided into 3 groups (the 3 columns) with 2 in each group. That way you get a mental image of what multiplication and division are, each time you look at the pictures.

Here's the array again:

Row 1:	1	2	3
Row 2:	4	5	6
Row 3:	7	8	9
Row 4:	10	11	12
Row 5:	13	14	15
Row 6:	16	17	18
Row 7:	19	20	21
Row 8:	22	23	24
Row 9:	25	26	27
Row 10:	28	29	30

Now please use it, if necessary, to give the answers to the following multiplication fact questions:

1. 3x5=
2. 3x1=
3. 3x4=
4. 1x3=
5. 3x9=
6. 3x3=
7. 4x3=
8. 3x10=
9. 3x2=
10. 2x3=
11. 5x3=
12. 9x3=
13. 3x6=
14. 10x3=
15. 8x3=
16. 3x7=
17. 6x3=
18. 3x8=
19. 7x3=

Learning the Math Facts

Here's the array for 3's one more time. First please use it to say the division facts, in order. Look at the rightmost column of the first row, and say, "3/3=1. 3/1=3." Look at the rightmost column of the second row, and say, "6/3=2; 6/2=3." Look at the rightmost column of the third row, where there is a 9, and say "9/3=3." (Only one division fact, since 9 is a square number.) Look at the 12 at the end of the 4th row, and say, "12/3=4; 12/4=3." And so forth.

You can use it to answer division problems. For example, let's say the problem is 18/3. We look down the rightmost column till we find 18. It's at the end of the 6th row, and we have 3 in each row. So 18/3=6. (And 18/6=3.)

Row 1:	1	2	3
Row 2:	4	5	6
Row 3:	7	8	9
Row 4:	10	11	12
Row 5:	13	14	15
Row 6:	16	17	18
Row 7:	19	20	21
Row 8:	22	23	24
Row 9:	25	26	27
Row 10:	28	29	30

Here are division problems to answer:

1. 3/3=
2. 27/3=
3. 12/3=
4. 21/3=
5. 6/3=
6. 15/3=
7. 24/3=
8. 30/3=
9. 9/3=
10. 18/3=
11. 3/1=
12. 12/4=
13. 15/3=
14. 6/2=
15. 15/5=
16. 27/9=
17. 30/3=
18. 21/7=
19. 6/3=
20. 24/8=

Chapter 20: Multiplication Fact Families Using Broken Number Line Arrays

Here's the array of 4's.

Row 1:	1	2	3	4
Row 2:	5	6	7	8
Row 3:	9	10	11	12
Row 4:	13	14	15	16
Row 5:	17	18	19	20
Row 6:	21	22	23	24
Row 7:	25	26	27	28
Row 8:	29	30	31	32
Row 9:	33	34	35	36
Row 10:	37	38	39	40

Please go through the rows from start to finish, say the four facts that are represented by the numbers up through that row. For row 1, you say: "4*1=4. 1*4=4. 4/4=1. 4/1=4."

After you're fast at that, pick rows at random and say the fact family members associated with them.

Now please get very fast at answering the following multiplication facts, using the array if you need to.

1. 4x1=
2. 4x6=
3. 4x3=
4. 4x10=
5. 4x8=
6. 4x2=
7. 4x5=
8. 4x9=
9. 4x4=
10. 4x7=
11. 1x4=
12. 4x4=
13. 8x4=
14. 3x4=
15. 6x4=
16. 10x4=
17. 5x4=
18. 7x4=
19. 2x4=
20. 9x4=

Learning the Math Facts

Here's the array of 4's again:

Row 1:   1   2   3   4
Row 2:   5   6   7   8
Row 3:   9   10   11   12
Row 4:   13   14   15   16
Row 5:   17   18   19   20
Row 6:   21   22   23   24
Row 7:   25   26   27   28
Row 8:   29   30   31   32
Row 9:   33   34   35   36
Row 10:   37   38   39   40

Please look at the array and say the division facts in order. You start with the end of the first row, and say, "4/1=4; 4/4=1." You look at the end of the second row, and you say, "8/2=4; 8/4=2." You look at the 12 at the end of the third row, and you say, "12/3=4; 12/4=3." And so forth.
Now please get as fast as you can with the following division facts:

1. 4/4=
2. 20/4=
3. 8/2=
4. 36/4=
5. 4/1=
6. 12/4=
7. 40/10=
8. 28/4=
9. 8/4=
10. 36/9=
11. 20/5=
12. 12/3=
13. 24/6=
14. 40/4=
15. 24/4=
16. 32/4=
17. 28/7=
18. 16/4=
19. 32/8=

Chapter 20: Multiplication Fact Families Using Broken Number Line Arrays

Here's an array of 5's:

Row 1:	1	2	3	4	5
Row 2:	6	7	8	9	10
Row 3:	11	12	13	14	15
Row 4:	16	17	18	19	20
Row 5:	21	22	23	24	25
Row 6:	26	27	28	29	30
Row 7:	31	32	33	34	35
Row 8:	36	37	38	39	40
Row 9:	41	42	43	44	45
Row 10:	46	47	48	49	50

Again, go from the first row through the tenth, saying the fact family members for each row. When you're fast at this, go in random order, saying the facts for randomly picked rows.

Practice the following multiplication facts, using the array if necessary. Aim for speed.

1. 5x6=
2. 5x1=
3. 5x5=
4. 5x2=
5. 5x7=
6. 5x9=
7. 5x4=
8. 5x3=
9. 5x10=
10. 5x8=
11. 4x5=
12. 1x5=
13. 6x5=
14. 9x5=
15. 3x5=
16. 5x5=
17. 10x5=
18. 7x5=
19. 2x5=
20. 8x5=

Here's the array of 5's again.

Row 1:	1	2	3	4	5
Row 2:	6	7	8	9	10
Row 3:	11	12	13	14	15
Row 4:	16	17	18	19	20
Row 5:	21	22	23	24	25
Row 6:	26	27	28	29	30
Row 7:	31	32	33	34	35
Row 8:	36	37	38	39	40
Row 9:	41	42	43	44	45
Row 10:	46	47	48	49	50

Please use the array of 5's to answer the following division questions:

1. 20/5=
2. 15/3=
3. 40/8=
4. 45/5=
5. 5/1=
6. 30/6=
7. 5/5=
8. 40/5=
9. 10/2=
10. 30/5=
11. 15/5=
12. 45/9=
13. 35/5=
14. 20/4=
15. 50/10=
16. 50/5=
17. 35/7=
18. 10/5=
19. 25/5=

Chapter 20: Multiplication Fact Families Using Broken Number Line Arrays

Now here's the array of 6's.

Row 1:	1	2	3	4	5	6
Row 2:	7	8	9	10	11	12
Row 3:	13	14	15	16	17	18
Row 4:	19	20	21	22	23	24
Row 5:	25	26	27	28	29	30
Row 6:	31	32	33	34	35	36
Row 7:	37	37	39	40	41	42
Row 8:	43	44	45	46	47	48
Row 9:	49	50	51	52	53	54
Row 10:	55	56	57	58	59	60

Please say the fact families for the 6s in order and in random order.

Then practice with these multiplication facts, looking at the array if you want.

1. 6*5=
2. 6*1=
3. 10*6=
4. 8*6=
5. 2*6=
6. 5*6=
7. 6*8=
8. 6*10=
9. 6*3=
10. 6*6=
11. 9*6=
12. 1*6=
13. 3*6=
14. 6*2=
15. 6*9=
16. 6*6=
17. 4*6=
18. 7*6=
19. 6*4=
20. 6*7=

Learning the Math Facts

Now here's the array of 6's again.

Row 1:	1	2	3	4	5	6
Row 2:	7	8	9	10	11	12
Row 3:	13	14	15	16	17	18
Row 4:	19	20	21	22	23	24
Row 5:	25	26	27	28	29	30
Row 6:	31	32	33	34	35	36
Row 7:	37	37	39	40	41	42
Row 8:	43	44	45	46	47	48
Row 9:	49	50	51	52	53	54
Row 10:	55	56	57	58	59	60

Please practice with the following division facts, looking at the array if you want.

1. 24/6=
2. 6/6=
3. 30/6=
4. 54/6=
5. 6/1=
6. 48/6=
7. 30/5=
8. 18/3=
9. 54/9=
10. 36/6=
11. 12/6=
12. 48/8=
13. 24/4=
14. 42/6=
15. 12/2=
16. 42/7=
17. 18/6=

Chapter 20: Multiplication Fact Families Using Broken Number Line Arrays

Now here's the array of 7's.

Row 1:	1	2	3	4	5	6	7
Row 2:	8	9	10	11	12	13	14
Row 3:	15	16	17	18	19	20	21
Row 4:	22	23	24	25	26	27	28
Row 5:	29	30	31	32	33	34	35
Row 6:	36	37	38	39	40	41	42
Row 7:	43	44	45	46	47	48	49
Row 8:	50	51	52	53	54	55	56
Row 9:	57	58	59	60	61	62	63
Row 10:	64	65	66	67	68	69	70

Please say the fact families for each row, first in order, then in random order. Keep going until you can do this fast.

Now, using the array, practice answering the following:

1. 7*5=
2. 7*7=
3. 1*7=
4. 6*7=
5. 7*2=
6. 9*7=
7. 7*8=
8. 3*7=
9. 7*3=
10. 5*7=
11. 7*10=
12. 2*7=
13. 7*1=
14. 8*7=
15. 7*7=
16. 10*7=
17. 7*4=
18. 7*9=
19. 4*7=
20. 7*6=

Learning the Math Facts

Now here's the array of 7's again.

Row 1:	1	2	3	4	5	6	7
Row 2:	8	9	10	11	12	13	14
Row 3:	15	16	17	18	19	20	21
Row 4:	22	23	24	25	26	27	28
Row 5:	29	30	31	32	33	34	35
Row 6:	36	37	38	39	40	41	42
Row 7:	43	44	45	46	47	48	49
Row 8:	50	51	52	53	54	55	56
Row 9:	57	58	59	60	61	62	63
Row 10:	64	65	66	67	68	69	70

Use the array, if you wish, to answer the following division questions:

1. 28/4=
2. 7/1=
3. 70/7=
4. 63/7=
5. 42/7=
6. 21/3=
7. 56/7=
8. 7/7=
9. 35/5=
10. 21/7=
11. 63/9=
12. 70/10=
13. 14/2=
14. 42/6=
15. 49/7=
16. 28/7=
17. 56/8=
18. 14/7=
19. 35/7=

Chapter 20: Multiplication Fact Families Using Broken Number Line Arrays

Here's the array formed by the number line, broken after every 8.

Row 1:	1	2	3	4	5	6	7	8
Row 2:	9	10	11	12	13	14	15	16
Row 3:	17	18	19	20	21	22	23	24
Row 4:	25	26	27	28	29	30	31	32
Row 5:	33	34	35	36	37	38	39	40
Row 6:	41	42	43	44	45	46	47	48
Row 7:	49	50	51	52	53	54	55	56
Row 8:	57	58	59	60	61	62	63	64
Row 9:	65	66	67	68	69	70	71	72
Row 10:	73	74	75	76	77	78	79	80

Please say the fact families for each row, first in order, then picking rows at random.

Now please practice with the following multiplication facts:

1. 8*6=
2. 8*1=
3. 3*8=
4. 6*8=
5. 8*8=
6. 8*4=
7. 8*9=
8. 8*7=
9. 10*8=
10. 2*8=
11. 8*2=
12. 8*5=
13. 8*10=
14. 4*8=
15. 1*8=
16. 8*8=
17. 7*8=
18. 5*8=
19. 8*3=
20. 9*8=

Here's the array for the 8s again:

Row 1:	1	2	3	4	5	6	7	8
Row 2:	9	10	11	12	13	14	15	16
Row 3:	17	18	19	20	21	22	23	24
Row 4:	25	26	27	28	29	30	31	32
Row 5:	33	34	35	36	37	38	39	40
Row 6:	41	42	43	44	45	46	47	48
Row 7:	49	50	51	52	53	54	55	56
Row 8:	57	58	59	60	61	62	63	64
Row 9:	65	66	67	68	69	70	71	72
Row 10:	73	74	75	76	77	78	79	80

Use the array, if you wish, to answer the following division questions:

1. 24/8=
2. 80/10=
3. 64/8=
4. 8/1=
5. 48/6=
6. 40/5=
7. 80/8=
8. 56/8=
9. 32/4=
10. 16/8=
11. 48/8=
12. 72/8=
13. 8/8=
14. 24/3=
15. 72/9=
16. 56/7=
17. 40/8=
18. 16/2=
19. 32/8=

Chapter 20: Multiplication Fact Families Using Broken Number Line Arrays

Finally, here's the array formed by breaking the number line after every 9:

Row 1:	1	2	3	4	5	6	7	8	9
Row 2:	10	11	12	13	14	15	16	17	18
Row 3:	19	20	21	22	23	24	25	26	27
Row 4:	28	29	30	31	32	33	34	35	36
Row 5:	37	38	39	40	41	42	43	44	45
Row 6:	46	47	48	49	50	51	52	53	54
Row 7:	55	56	57	58	59	60	61	62	63
Row 8:	64	65	66	67	68	69	70	71	72
Row 9:	73	74	75	76	77	78	79	80	81
Row 10:	82	83	84	85	86	87	88	89	90

Please say the fact families associated with each row, first in order, and then for a random order of rows. Keep going till you can do this fast.

Now please practice with the following multiplication facts:

1. 9*4=
2. 4*9=
3. 6*9=
4. 9*1=
5. 9*9=
6. 1*9=
7. 9*6=
8. 9*3=
9. 2*9=
10. 9*5=
11. 9*10=
12. 10*9=
13. 9*7=
14. 7*9=
15. 5*9=
16. 8*9=
17. 3*9=
18. 9*2=
19. 9*8=
20. 9*9=

Here's the array for the 9's again:

Row 1:	1	2	3	4	5	6	7	8	9
Row 2:	10	11	12	13	14	15	16	17	18
Row 3:	19	20	21	22	23	24	25	26	27
Row 4:	28	29	30	31	32	33	34	35	36
Row 5:	37	38	39	40	41	42	43	44	45
Row 6:	46	47	48	49	50	51	52	53	54
Row 7:	55	56	57	58	59	60	61	62	63
Row 8:	64	65	66	67	68	69	70	71	72
Row 9:	73	74	75	76	77	78	79	80	81
Row 10:	82	83	84	85	86	87	88	89	90

Now please practice the following division facts, using the array as necessary:

1. 9/9=
2. 72/9=
3. 90/10=
4. 63/7=
5. 45/5=
6. 90/9=
7. 36/4=
8. 72/8=
9. 54/6=
10. 81/9=
11. 27/3=
12. 9/1=
13. 45/9=
14. 63/9=
15. 18/9=
16. 54/9=
17. 27/9=
18. 36/9=
19. 18/2=

Chapter 21: Visualizing Multiplication Facts With The Traditional Multiplication Table

I used broken number lines for you to visualize the multiplication facts. There's another way to view them, which is commonly called "the multiplication table."

1	2	3	4	5	6	7	8	9	10
2	4	6	8	10	12	14	16	18	20
3	6	9	12	15	18	21	24	27	30
4	8	12	16	20	24	28	32	36	40
5	10	15	20	25	30	35	40	45	50
6	12	18	24	30	36	42	48	54	60
7	14	21	28	35	42	49	56	63	70
8	16	24	32	40	48	56	64	72	80
9	18	27	36	45	54	63	72	81	90
10	20	30	40	50	60	70	80	90	100

This is a very interesting table, in many ways. Let's look at it and notice some things.

First, you can make it by skip counting across the rows: first by 1s, then 2s, then 3s, and so forth. When you've written the skip counts for

Learning the Math Facts

the 10 rows, look at the columns, and lo and behold, there are the same skip counts written in the columns! The table has all the skip-counts you need to know for multiplication.

Another thing to notice about this table is that you can retrieve any multiplication fact by seeing where a certain row crosses a certain column. For example, 3 x 4, look in the third row and the fourth column. You find 12 there. You could also look in the fourth row and the third column; you find 12 there also.

Do you remember that I used the broken number line arrays so that when you practiced with, for example, 2 x 3, you would see two groups of three things, and also 3 groups of two things, for a total of 6 things altogether? In the traditional multiplication table, you can also see those things – it's just that it isn't so clear how many you're dealing with, because we don't count them by ones.

1	**2**	**3**	4	5	6	7	8	9	10
2	**4**	**6**	8	10	12	14	16	18	20
3	6	9	12	15	18	21	24	27	30
4	8	12	16	20	24	28	32	36	40
5	10	15	20	25	30	35	40	45	50
6	12	18	24	30	36	42	48	54	60
7	14	21	28	35	42	49	56	63	70
8	16	24	32	40	48	56	64	72	80
9	18	27	36	45	54	63	72	81	90
10	20	30	40	50	60	70	80	90	100

Let's look at how the multiplication table represents 3 x 2 (or 2 x 3). In the table above, I've put into thicker print (or "bolded") the first three columns of the first 2 rows. There is 6, where the 2nd row crosses the 3rd column. How many numbers have I bolded? There are six of them – two groups of three, or three groups of two. Unlike with our broken number lines, it isn't so obvious that there are six, because we don't see them counted by ones. But when we see the answer "6," looking at the

Chapter 21: Visualizing Multiplication Facts With The Traditional Multiplication Table

block of numbers formed by the first 2 rows and the first 3 columns, and ignoring all the rest, we are actually looking at 6 things, that is, 6 numbers. This is true for any number in the table! When we go to the 9th row and the 8th column, and see 72, there are actually 72 numbers in the rectangle formed by the first 9 rows and the first 8 columns.

One of the main ideas of this book has been: do a lot of drilling on math facts with some sort of table or diagram in front of you that allows you to get the answers from it, and that also gives you a visual image of why the fact is true. Only after you've done a lot of this do I ask you to practice with just "squiggles," or numerals without the pictures that go along with the facts.

Let's use the multiplication table of this chapter to do some more drilling on multiplication and division facts. Here are different steps you can take.

1. For any row, or for all the rows, you can practice saying the multiplication facts in order. The first row is the 1's row; you'd say: 1*1=1, 1*2=2, 1*3=3, 1*4=4, and so forth. The second row is the 2s row; you'd say 2*1=2, 2*2=4, 2*3=6, 2*4=8, 2*5=10, and so forth. As you do this, hopefully your brain can be aware for example that when you are saying 2*5 you are looking at 2 rows, and the first 5 in each row, so you are looking at 2 groups of 5 things (or 5 groups of 2 things).

2. For any row, or for all the rows, you can practice saying the fact families in order. For example, for row 7, you start out like this: "7*1=7; 1*7=7; 7/7=1; 7/1=7. 7*2=14; 2*7=14; 14/2=7; 14/7=2."

3. For any row, you can practice saying the multiplication facts or the fact families in random order. For example, for row 6, doing the fact families, you might start out saying something like, "6*3=18; 3*6=18; 18/6=3; 18/3=6. 6*9=54; 9*6=54; 54/6=9; 54/9=6."

4. You can look over the whole table for the multiplication and division facts you are shakiest with, and say the fact families for those.

For example, if you're shaky on 7*9 and 6*8, you might start out "7*9=63; 9*7=63; 63/7=9; 63/9=7. 6*8=48; 8*6=48; 48/6=8; 48/8=6."

    5. Sometimes division facts don't get the emphasis they should. Another way to use this table is to look at any row and say only the division facts, in order and then in random order. For example, with the 9th row, in order, you start off "9/9=1, 9/1=9; 18/9=2; 18/2=9. 27/9=3; 27/3=9." For random order, you might start off: "54/9=6; 54/6=9. 36/9=4; 36/4=9."

Chapter 22: Practicing Multiplication and Division Facts Using Numerals Only

Now it's time to practice multiplication and division facts without pictures or tables to help out. Practice with the following 36 basic multiplication facts. Get as fast as you can.

1. 4*2=
2. 9*6=
3. 8*5=
4. 9*4=
5. 5*3=
6. 8*4=
7. 6*5=
8. 7*2=
9. 7*6=
10. 9*2=
11. 8*3=
12. 2*2=
13. 6*2=
14. 9*3=
15. 8*6=
16. 7*4=
17. 5*2=
18. 9*5=
19. 7*7=
20. 8*7=
21. 3*3=
22. 8*8=
23. 9*7=
24. 4*3=
25. 6*3=
26. 3*2=
27. 9*9=
28. 7*3=
29. 8*2=
30. 5*4=
31. 9*8=
32. 7*5=
33. 6*6=
34. 6*4=
35. 4*4=
36. 5*5=

Learning the Math Facts

Now here are some division facts to practice on.

1. 8/4=
2. 54/9=
3. 40/8=
4. 36/9=
5. 15/5=
6. 32/8=
7. 30/6=
8. 14/7=
9. 42/7=
10. 18/9=
11. 24/8=
12. 4/2=
13. 12/6=
14. 27/9=
15. 48/8=
16. 28/7=
17. 10/5=
18. 45/9=
19. 49/7=
20. 56/8=
21. 9/3=
22. 64/8=
23. 63/9=
24. 12/4=
25. 18/6=
26. 6/3=
27. 81/9=
28. 21/7=
29. 16/8=
30. 20/5=
31. 72/9=
32. 35/7=
33. 36/6=
34. 24/6=
35. 16/4=
36. 25/5=

Chapter 22: Practicing Multiplication and Division Facts Using Numerals Only

Here are the division facts, using the other member of the fact family for each division fact used in the previous list.

1. 8/2=
2. 54/6=
3. 40/5=
4. 36/4=
5. 15/3=
6. 32/4=
7. 30/5=
8. 14/2=
9. 42/6=
10. 18/2=
11. 24/3=
12. 4/2=
13. 12/2=
14. 27/3=
15. 48/6=
16. 28/4=
17. 10/2=
18. 45/5=
19. 49/7=
20. 56/7=
21. 9/3=
22. 64/8=
23. 63/7=
24. 12/3=
25. 18/3=
26. 6/2=
27. 81/9=
28. 21/3=
29. 16/2=
30. 20/4=
31. 72/8=
32. 35/5=
33. 36/6=
34. 24/4=
35. 16/4=
36. 25/5=

Learning the Math Facts

Here are multiplication and division facts, in random order:

1. 15/5=
2. 5*5=
3. 9/3=
4. 9*5=
5. 36/4=
6. 6/3=
7. 2*5=
8. 9*9=
9. 5*9=
10. 8/2=
11. 3*7=
12. 12/4=
13. 63/7=
14. 8*8=
15. 24/4=
16. 40/5=
17. 9*6=
18. 18/3=
19. 48/8=
20. 6*5=
21. 63/9=
22. 36/9=
23. 7*4=
24. 8/4=
25. 9*9=
26. 27/9=
27. 32/4=
28. 48/6=
29. 6*8=
30. 12/2=
31. 30/6=
32. 5*5=
33. 4*8=
34. 5*4=
35. 21/3=
36. 2*2=
37. 72/9=
38. 45/5=
39. 6*3=
40. 3*4=
41. 8*4=
42. 7*3=
43. 6/2=
44. 7*2=
45. 6*2=
46. 3*6=
47. 2*2=
48. 12/6=
49. 3*9=
50. 12/3=
51. 18/9=
52. 56/7=
53. 18/6=
54. 81/9=
55. 7*6=
56. 42/7=
57. 18/2=
58. 9*3=
59. 72/8=
60. 6*6=
61. 4*2=
62. 4*6=
63. 5*8=
64. 3*5=
65. 2*4=
66. 64/8=
67. 81/9=
68. 3*3=
69. 4*4=
70. 54/9=
71. 8*7=
72. 2*8=
73. 35/7=
74. 5*6=
75. 16/2=
76. 4*4=
77. 9/3=
78. 9*4=
79. 8*8=
80. 36/6=
81. 49/7=
82. 4/2=
83. 7*7=
84. 5*2=
85. 5*7=

Chapter 22: Practicing Multiplication and Division Facts Using Numerals Only

86. 4*5=
87. 9*7=
88. 7*9=
89. 14/2=
90. 4/2=
91. 3*3=
92. 8*2=
93. 16/8=
94. 6*4=
95. 45/9=
96. 42/6=
97. 28/7=
98. 2*6=
99. 2*9=
100. 15/3=
101. 24/8=
102. 32/8=
103. 5*3=
104. 28/4=
105. 56/8=
106. 40/8=
107. 4*9=
108. 25/5=
109. 9*2=
110. 6*7=
111. 24/6=
112. 27/3=
113. 3*8=
114. 8*9=
115. 8*6=
116. 36/6=
117. 7*7=
118. 16/4=
119. 24/3=
120. 25/5=
121. 9*8=
122. 10/5=
123. 20/4=
124. 2*3=
125. 3*2=
126. 6*9=
127. 10/2=
128. 30/5=
129. 20/5=
130. 54/6=
131. 64/8=
132. 35/5=
133. 49/7=
134. 8*3=
135. 6*6=
136. 7*8=
137. 2*7=
138. 7*5=
139. 4*3=
140. 14/7=
141. 4*7=
142. 21/7=
143. 16/4=
144. 8*5=

Learning the Math Facts

Chapter 23: Practice With Random Math Facts

Now let's practice with randomly mixed up math facts of all four operations.

1. 7*10=
2. 4*9=
3. 7*7=
4. 4*4=
5. 16-10=
6. 9*3=
7. 9+1=
8. 7/1=
9. 4-1=
10. 13-6=
11. 35/7=
12. 36/4=
13. 2-1=
14. 5/5=
15. 3+10=
16. 5*8=
17. 7*9=
18. 6/3=
19. 9*4=
20. 0+2=
21. 6+1=
22. 2*9=
23. 2*10=
24. 12/2=
25. 7+9=
26. 3*5=
27. 4*8=
28. 40/5=
29. 6*5=
30. 1*2=
31. 3*0=
32. 28/4=
33. 15-7=
34. 2+2=
35. 9+3=
36. 1*2=
37. 4+0=
38. 20-10=
39. 1*4=
40. 18/3=
41. 9+7=
42. 14-9=
43. 2+1=
44. 8*5=
45. 4*4=
46. 25/5=
47. 11-10=
48. 19-10=
49. 40/8=
50. 14/2=
51. 72/8=
52. 9+10=
53. 9/3=
54. 4*6=
55. 2+4=
56. 0+0=
57. 2+1=
58. 21/3=
59. 5-2=
60. 10*8=
61. 40/8=
62. 17-10=
63. 6+8=
64. 6*2=
65. 4*8=
66. 6+3=
67. 8-2=
68. 7+9=
69. 18-8=
70. 0/3=
71. 0+6=
72. 8*9=
73. 7-4=
74. 18/9=
75. 1+0=
76. 7-2=
77. 6-5=
78. 1-1=
79. 42/7=
80. 1+4=
81. 4+8=
82. 5-3=
83. 6+1=
84. 3/1=
85. 5-2=
86. 3+10=
87. 6+5=
88. 9*1=
89. 8-2=
90. 0*4=
91. 6*5=
92. 32/8=
93. 10-2=
94. 12/3=
95. 8-1=
96. 4*7=
97. 12/3=
98. 10+7=
99. 3-1=
100. 16-10=
101. 1*2=
102. 16-8=

Learning the Math Facts

103. 10+9=
104. 5/5=
105. 10*7=
106. 16-7=
107. 7*6=
108. 8+3=
109. 9-7=
110. 9+6=
111. 4/1=
112. 0/1=
113. 7+3=
114. 6-5=
115. 11-9=
116. 5-1=
117. 3*5=
118. 9+3=
119. 9*1=
120. 5+4=
121. 48/8=
122. 4+1=
123. 28/4=
124. 40/4=
125. 0+0=
126. 6+8=
127. 0/9=
128. 6-1=
129. 12/2=
130. 40/4=
131. 8*3=
132. 7-7=
133. 28/4=
134. 8+9=
135. 10+0=
136. 13-8=
137. 8*8=
138. 1+8=
139. 32/8=
140. 2*5=

141. 50/5=
142. 0*10=
143. 18/9=
144. 2+6=
145. 4+10=
146. 10/2=
147. 9-1=
148. 28/7=
149. 6+3=
150. 4*7=
151. 70/7=
152. 9+7=
153. 5+6=
154. 0+7=
155. 4-1=
156. 7+2=
157. 9*2=
158. 9-6=
159. 4+0=
160. 7*8=
161. 20/10=
162. 3*1=
163. 16/2=
164. 27/3=
165. 0*1=
166. 54/9=
167. 30/6=
168. 20-10=
169. 11-8=
170. 17-9=
171. 20/2=
172. 16/4=
173. 13-8=
174. 5+2=
175. 5*5=
176. 42/6=
177. 14/7=
178. 5*8=

179. 5-2=
180. 1*5=
181. 4-3=
182. 8+6=
183. 18/6=
184. 20/5=
185. 7/1=
186. 2*3=
187. 5+2=
188. 12/6=
189. 7*8=
190. 7*10=
191. 2+9=
192. 9+3=
193. 1*10=
194. 4+8=
195. 7+3=
196. 8-4=
197. 9/9=
198. 60/10=
199. 9*7=
200. 13-7=
201. 0+0=
202. 8*3=
203. 1+1=
204. 5*6=
205. 2*5=
206. 6+8=
207. 1+4=
208. 0+0=
209. 14/2=
210. 0+7=
211. 7+7=
212. 9+10=
213. 6+6=
214. 1+0=
215. 3+2=
216. 80/10=

Chapter 23: Practice With Random Math Facts

217. 5-3=
218. 11-3=
219. 16-6=
220. 3*2=
221. 9-8=
222. 4+4=
223. 12/4=
224. 4*3=
225. 36/4=
226. 8-7=
227. 10*7=
228. 4+10=
229. 3*3=
230. 0+9=
231. 6*4=
232. 6+5=
233. 15-7=
234. 2+0=
235. 2*1=
236. 8-3=
237. 2+6=
238. 7+10=
239. 45/5=
240. 6*5=
241. 0/7=
242. 8*6=
243. 8-5=
244. 9+4=
245. 19-10=
246. 2+8=
247. 3+6=
248. 16/8=
249. 0*3=
250. 30/6=
251. 8*4=
252. 63/9=
253. 9+10=
254. 4/4=

255. 60/6=
256. 8+10=
257. 9+4=
258. 90/10=
259. 19-9=
260. 0*0=
261. 10/2=
262. 7*2=
263. 0/9=
264. 15/5=
265. 3+7=
266. 1+6=
267. 10*3=
268. 3+4=
269. 7+10=
270. 12/6=
271. 2*10=
272. 1*1=
273. 18/3=
274. 3+9=
275. 20/2=
276. 4+8=
277. 10/2=
278. 1*2=
279. 3+1=
280. 1+3=
281. 8-1=
282. 63/9=
283. 15-6=
284. 17-9=
285. 100/10=
286. 3*8=
287. 4-3=
288. 0/4=
289. 16-7=
290. 14-9=
291. 9*7=
292. 27/3=

293. 10*5=
294. 10*3=
295. 7+9=
296. 8+9=
297. 6/6=
298. 2*4=
299. 12/6=
300. 9-2=
301. 10/10=
302. 19-10=
303. 10*6=
304. 9+0=
305. 18/6=
306. 6*2=
307. 7-2=
308. 12-9=
309. 70/10=
310. 5+2=
311. 10-8=
312. 1*8=
313. 30/5=
314. 27/3=
315. 1*0=
316. 8*4=
317. 15-8=
318. 2*0=
319. 0*2=
320. 0*9=
321. 2+9=
322. 9+4=
323. 4*4=
324. 72/8=
325. 3*10=
326. 7+1=
327. 7*2=
328. 1*4=
329. 6-1=
330. 7-7=

Learning the Math Facts

331. 20/10=
332. 36/9=
333. 13-5=
334. 17-7=
335. 10+2=

336. 0/6=
337. 32/8=
338. 12/3=
339. 10/2=
340. 9-9=

341. 0*6=
342. 6-6=
343. 5*8=
344. 9-1=
345. 1+8=

Index

2 pluses with dominoes 53
3 pluses with dominoes 54
36 addition facts to memorize 25
adding zero 23
adding one 23
adding ten 24
addition facts page with answers 25
addition table 58
addition work for multiplication 75
arrays for multiplication and division 108
asterisk (to mean "multiplied by" 12
aversions, conditioned 8
borrowing in subtraction 76
broken number line 20
broken number line arrays, for multiplication and division 108
broken number line page, addition 38
broken number line page, addition and subtraction 50
broken number lines 29
broken number lines 31
broken number lines adding whole row with 35
broken number lines for multiplication 88
carrying in addition 75
column 18
commutative law of addition 23
commutative law of multiplication 82
dividing a number by itself 102
dividing by ten 102
division by one 102
division by zero, not allowed 102
division, questions answered by 98

division, reducing memorization of 101
division, relation to multiplication 97
domino 19
dominoes for 8 pluses 56
dominoes for 9 pluses 56
doubles, adding 65
drill, 36 addition facts 72
drill, 36 subtraction facts 73
drilling methods with addition table 59
drilling with visual aid 127
fact families with dominoes 51
fact families, multiplication and division 104
fact families, with multiplication and division 101
fact family 40
fun, making practices 16
inverse, division of multiplication 100
make 10's, adding 71
make five subtraction facts 45
memorization in multiplication, reducing 82
memorization, reducing for subtraction 39
memorization, reducing with division facts 101
memorizing, reducing for addition facts 22
minus five subtraction with broken number line 48
multiplication as repeated addition 75
multiplication facts, answers supplied 85
multiplication table, traditional 125
multiplying by one 84
multiplying by ten 85
multiplying by zero 84
multiplying using broken number lines 88
multiplying with ordinary number line 87
number line 19
number line, adding with 27

Index

number lines without the lines 20
number sense 6
numerals only, practicing multiplication and division with 129
numerals, practicing addition with 61
one aparts, adding 66
one, multiplying by 84
order doesn't make a difference in multiplication 82
order doesn't make a difference 22
ordinary number line, multiplying with 87
ordinary number line, subtracting with 43
page, broken number line addition and subtraction 50
perfect squares 91
plus 2's, practicing 63
plus 8's, adding 69
plus 9's, adding 68
practice with using subtraction rules 42
practice, role of 14
practicing 36 division facts 130
practicing 36 multiplication facts 129
practicing division rules 103
practicing multiplication and division, random order 132
questions answered by division 98
random math facts, 4 operations 135
regrouping in addition 75
regrouping in subtraction 76
relaxing, while going fast 16
repetition-tolerance 14
row 18
seeing how big numbers are 18
self-monitoring 15
skip-counting sequences 76
skip-counting songs 81
squares, perfect 91

steps for practicing multiplication 91
stress, from time pressure 16
subtracting zero 40
subtracting one 41
subtracting ten 41
subtracting ones' place number 41
subtracting, with ordinary number line 43
ten, multiplying by 85
timing methods 9
timing, when not to 8
traditional multiplication table 125
two aparts, adding 70
zero, dividing it by a number 101
zero, multiplying by 84
zero, not dividing by 101

www.ingramcontent.com/pod-product-compliance
Lightning Source LLC
Chambersburg PA
CBHW081457040426
42446CB00016B/3282